SHOPPING BAG LADIES

SHOPPING BAG LADIES

Homeless Women Speak About Their Lives

BY ANN MARIE ROUSSEAU

Preface By Alix Kates Shulman

The Pilgrim Press
New York

Library of Congress Cataloging in Publication Data

Rousseau, Ann Marie, 1946-
   Shopping bag ladies.

   1. Homeless women—United States. 2. Homeless
women—Services for—United States.   I. Title.
HV1445.R68   305.4′8   81-407
ISBN 0-8298-0413-7
ISBN 0-8298-0603-2 (pbk.)   AACR1

The United Church Board for Homeland
Ministries, the parent agency of The Pilgrim
Press, has mounted a program to assist homeless
women. For more information, contact: Homeless
Women Project, United Church Board for
Homeland Ministries, 132 West 31 St.,
New York, NY 10001.

Pictures printed by Kaplan

Cover and book design by Pamela Vassil

The Pilgrim Press, 132 West 31 Street,
New York, New York 10001

TO JOAN, MARION, BERNARD AND WILLIAM ROUSSEAU

I am indebted to many people for their help, support, and advice in the making of this book. Ellen Baxter and Kim Hopper of Community Service Society offered me unpublished research, read my manuscript, and shared tips on locating people and places where the homeless stayed. They more than anyone else truly understood the gritty problems, difficulties, and frustrations I encountered in this work. Papers by Keith Schwam, Sharon Winget, and Jane Haggstrom were important sources of critical information. Jane was also a good friend and fellow researcher. Len Speier, my lawyer, friend, and fellow photographer helped in more ways than can be described. Kris Pidkameny and Tim Rollins deciphered and transcribed miles of tapes that were often of poor quality, and impossible to hear.

In every city, I spent hours talking to the social workers, directors, and workers at shelters and centers for the homeless. I owe great thanks to all of them for the time and energy they gave me. In Boston, I wish to thank Val Lanier of Rosie's Place, Karen McCarthy of Pine Street, Paula Ehelbrick of the Salvation Army; in San Francisco, Kitty Ryan of the San Francisco County Hospital, Jim Grace of the Gospel Mission, Margaret and David Croxford of the Life Line Mission, Butch Keith, Father Floyd Lotito, L.F.M., and Beth Payne of St. Anthony's Dining Hall, Edith Kaplan of the Salvation Army, Phil Stolz of the Mobile Assistance Program, and Pam Lee. In New York, my appreciation goes to Sister Maria Angeline Rasomilay and Bob Nesbit of Star of the Sea, the sisters at the Dwelling Place, Eileen Egan of Mary House, and Robert White, Catherine Hillery, Robert Gibson, successive directors of the Women's Shelter while I worked there.

Janet and John Hixon, Barbara and Al Lash, Larry Bowser, Peter Golden, Orie Fontaine and David Maclay gave me their friendship and most importantly a place to stay in their respective cities. Joan Rousseau, Dale Leifeste, Joan Reutershan, Donna Simonie, Lilly Hoffman, Ruth Meyers and Stephanie Golden read and reread the manuscript through its many transformations. Photographers J. Ross Baughman and Susan Meiselas provided inspiration and thoughtful criticism. I wish to thank my editor, Esther Cohen, for the creative energy and effort she put towards this book, and for her patience and tolerance through some difficult times. My deepest gratitude goes finally to the many homeless women who allowed me into their lives. My thoughts continue to be with them.

ACKNOWLEDGMENTS

PHOTOGRAPHS

INTERVIEWS

CONTENTS

9

Shopping bag ladies: Aging women with swollen ankles and ulcerated feet, toting bags, shuffling slowly across the street, poking into garbage cans, slumped on a park bench, dozing in doorways, sprawling across library steps, huddled among their possessions in the dreary waiting rooms of train and bus stations. Poor, sick, lonely, old, afraid.

Impoverished, homeless women have been with us for as long as there have been urban poor, but only recently have they appeared in large enough numbers to enter the public consciousness as a group apart—part puzzle, part pity, part threat. Fearful or finicky people turn aside when they see one coming, the fastidious sometimes report them to the police, youths harass them, thieves rob them, psychopaths burn and strangle them. Now that the term for them is gaining currency, the curious wonder who they are, how they got that way, why they live on the street, what they carry in those mysterious shopping bags, and if perhaps they themselves may one day become one of them.

But for most people, homeless women remain, as they have always been, essentially invisible. There are now thousands of homeless women inhabiting our large cities (approximately 4,000 in New York City in 1979, by one estimate, and increasing steadily[1]), but most of them pass their days unseen by the rest of us. To the extent that they are noticed at all, they are commonly seen as eccentric characters, strangely dressed hags, solitary half-mad collectors who spend their days rummaging through trash and making free use of the city as if, in the words of sociologist Jennifer Hand, "they owned the place."[2] Popular jokes and stories portray the shopping bag lady as feisty, rebellious, independent, and sometimes even rich, hiding untold treasures in her shopping bags—a woman whose special brand of madness has led her to prefer a free life on the street to the dependencies of welfare or the restrictions of responsible social life. (In Kurt Vonnegut Jr.'s latest novel, a shopping bag lady turns out to be the richest woman in the world!)

There may be a trace of truth in this portrait. After all, life on the streets is so hazardous that survivors must indeed be tough, exerting what one observer has called the negative strength of refusal in order to preserve "a small secret core of personal integrity."[3] Many homeless women do have a history of mental illness. Although most street dwellers are destitute and find it impossible to hold on to property of any monetary value, one rare shopping bag lady was discovered to have bankbooks worth $20,000 after she was set aflame by four teenaged boys in 1978. And bizarrely dressed women talking to themselves or pushing carts piled high with bags through the streets do exist and are in fact more likely to attract attention from media and passersby than the quiet women who disappear in the urban glut.

Nevertheless, this popular picture is distorted. I have just spent a year as a volunteer in a program serving shopping bag ladies in the Times Square area of New York City, two years investigating the lives of these women for a novel I recently completed, and my experience confirms what Ann Marie Rousseau's unflinchingly honest photographs and interviews reveal. Most homeless women live on the street not by preference or personal destiny, but because they dread ending their lives in institutions and are too poor or otherwise handicapped to obtain safe housing. A sudden crisis—a fire, a crime, an illness, an eviction, a death—may land a woman on the street, and once there, she may find her choices as reduced as her circumstances. As one expert observes, "to obtain and keep a home in our society is a complex and competitive matter which demands a clear mind, a high degree of responsibility, and money.[4]

Money. Too old, sick, or unskilled to work, many homeless women are simply unable to amass the documents or otherwise negotiate the bewildering bureaucratic maze of appointments (frequently scheduled simultaneously in different parts of town), application forms, interviews, medical checks, and follow-ups that are required of those who receive public assistance. As many of them know from experience, one lost document, one missed appointment, one wrong answer, and their case may be closed, making the very effort to comply seem futile. Without money, they have little choice but to live off the bounty of the street. As for those who do manage to get public assistance, their checks may get lost, their money may run out before the rent is due and they may find themselves evicted, the only rooms they can afford may seem more dangerous than the streets. In rooming houses and welfare hotels where the locks on the doors have been repeatedly forced, where the elevators and stairwells are setups for muggings, where fires are frequent, where your neighbors may well be addicts or professional thieves, you may view life on the street as actually safer. Or there may simply be no affordable rooms available. Low-rent city apartments and welfare hotels are rapidly disappearing, mainly through lucrative conversions to housing for the well-

PREFACE

10

to-do, inflationary rents, or deterioration.[5] When faced with the choice between spending most of your limited funds on rent and having something to spend on food, people may be forced to choose food.

But it is really not surprising that the public either fails to see homeless women at all, or else holds a distorted picture of them, when even specialists on the needy have persistently turned their attention elsewhere. While library shelves are full of books devoted to homeless men, subdivided into categories ranging from skid row bums to vagrants and tramps, while government commissions have been appointed to study them all through the century, as yet there is only a handful of studies of homeless women, mostly short, local, and very recent.[6] "Skid row men in the United States have been carefully and extensively studied for more than eighty years and are very well known to sociologists," writes sociologist Theodore Caplow, "but homeless women are something of a sociological mystery."[7] This situation is especially distressing when in recent years the increase in population of the elderly has amounted to a virtual explosion and is growing every year, particularly for elderly women living alone.[8] Nor is it surprising, given the invisibility of homeless women, that public facilities for them are meager compared to those available to men, though women comprise a majority of the elderly poor and receive far less money than men, both during their working years and after retirement. Of the beds available for a night to the New York City homeless through city emergency shelters, for example, shockingly few are allotted to women. The Men's Shelter can accommodate a seemingly unlimited number of applicants through its policy of distributing "chits" for beds in lodging houses and its offer of meals, medical treatment, clothing, and counseling to non-residents. The Women's Shelter, by contrast, has only about fifty beds (plus another ninety-seven at an annex), has strict admissions requirements, offers services only to its few residents, and since 1975 has turned away three quarters of its applicants.[9]

Why have homeless women received so much less attention and care than homeless men? Principally, of course, for the same reasons that women everywhere in our society have received relatively little public attention, whether from public servants, historians, employers, legislators, or shapers of consciousness: In a society in which women have little power, their lives are considered unimportant compared to the lives of men. Indeed, there may also be certain differences in the life-styles of homeless women and homeless men that tend to reinforce women's invisibility. According to sociologist Jennifer Hand, shopping bag ladies are urban economic outsiders who "live in nooks, crannies and niches," using public or semi-public places "for their own practical purposes," and differ from homeless men by using ploys derived from specifically female roles, like shopping, sorting, selecting, collecting, to gain access to urban facilities.[10] Then, too, women, being more vulnerable and fearful on the street than men, naturally have strong reason to try to be as inconspicuous as possible, while men, generally perceived as more threatening than women, have less reason to do so. (Studies of the homeless have confirmed, for example, that men more often congregate on the street to drink, while women drink alone.[11]) But these differences in the daily lives of impoverished women and men living alone in large cities are hardly great enough to account for the persistent relative invisibility of women. Historically, homeless men have been romanticized in American consciousness in a way that women have not. The vanished society of hobos, with their songs, secret language, anarchist leanings, and social traditions; the world of the vagrant and tramp with their bundles on a stick, airily associated with the romance of the Open Road celebrated by writers from Whitman to Kerouac; even the harsh urban world of the skid row bum with its grim fantasies of male camaraderie—these falsely romanticized male worlds that have periodically captured the American imagination have rarely extended to women. "The typical skid row population is exclusively male, except for the peripheral presence of a few landladies, prostitutes, and transients," writes Theodore Caplow;[12] and Nels Anderson, in his 1923 classic study of homeless men, *The Hobo*, writes with assurance, "Tramping is a man's game. Few women are ever found on the Road."[13] Indeed, the words "tramp" and "bum" applied to women do not even imply homelessness, as they do for men; a woman tramp is simply a "sexually promiscuous" woman, one who wanders not from place to place but from man to man. Traditionally, the groups of oppressed women that have been romanticized into visibility, however distorted the images, are prostitutes and even perhaps witches, but not the homeless.

In recent years, however, a romance does seem to have been slowly building up around the image of the solitary shopping bag lady and her bags. Magazine pieces, editorials, plays, poems, photo spreads have begun to appear not on the homeless in general but on shopping bag ladies in particular. I think this new, somewhat nervous interest in the odd lone woman who lugs her mysterious burden through the streets springs from a growing fear many women have for their own old age in a society where the traditional familial sources of women's security are in flux and where so many women can expect to wind up poor and alone. In 1974 the feminist newspaper *Majority Report* devoted an entire issue to shopping bag ladies. There are men, too, of course, who spend their days searching through trash for salvagings, and even a few who wheel bags through the city in baby carriages. Still, in our culture, the ubiquitous bag—women's indispensable gear, whether purse, tote, or shopping bag—remains an almost universal female sign, connecting "us" with "them." It is not always easy to tell homeless women from other women. Even women with comfortable homes commonly carry around in their bags supplies for every occasion, from papers and pills to folding umbrellas and food. Nor is it only the homeless in this commodity-obsessed society who spend much of their time collecting, shopping around, squirreling things away. Nevertheless, there is a great difference between those who carry shopping bags for convenience and those who must—the difference of extreme poverty and isolation. While most of us have cupboards, drawers, closets, and some even have attics, cellars, and safes in which to store our worldly goods, the homeless have only their shopping bags. Everything they own must travel with them. (No wonder the bags are sometimes cartons, a suitcase, a cart, like some

pictured in this book.) In 1973 it was a revelation to me when, reading Sharon Curtin's *Nobody Ever Died of Old Age,* I discovered that many people who carry their possessions around with them do so because they live in such vulnerable quarters that they are simply afraid to leave their things behind when they leave their rooms.

As one gradually begins to understand the extremely tenuous circumstances in which these people live, the less mysterious become their bags, the less strange their behavior, and the less invisible their lives. It is the great virtue of Ann Marie Rousseau's stark yet gripping book that it treats these women not as a collection of grotesques, but as part of suffering, impoverished America. Though it is difficult to look at some of these pictures because of the suffering they reveal, it is also impossible to look away or to hurry past with averted eyes, as even the compassionate among us are tempted to do when encountering these lone women on the street. In the pages of this book we can confront them in the true conditions of their lives, as the author and her camera have done. Seeing them through Rousseau's humane photographs and forthright interviews as real people, we can face the ulcerated feet, the endless search for food, the weariness, the waiting, even the invisibility these women normally suffer. (Notice how few passersby in these pictures seem to look at the women, even when one of them is changing her clothes on a crowded street.) If this oddly beautiful, disturbing book can bring ordinarily unseen lives into the light of consciousness and leave us with a new set of permanent images, then it shall have performed for all of us the service of art. —*Alix Kates Shulman*

1 Estimate of the Manhattan Bowery Corporation Report to the Fund for the City of New York, "Shopping Bag Ladies: Homeless Women," April 1, 1979, p. 8.

2 Jennifer Hand, "Shopping Bag Ladies: A Study in Interstitial Urban Behavior," paper presented to the Society for the Study of Social Problems, New York City, August 1976, p. 6.

3 Stephanie Golden, "The Transforming Tree: Finding Our Roots in the Homeless Women," *Conditions: Four,* Winter 1979, p. 93.

4 Manhattan Bowery Corporation Report, p. 3.

5 According to a report of the New York City Department of Social Services, "The Diminishing Resource: Lower-Priced Hotels in New York City," 1979, there were 63% fewer hotels offering rooms at $50 a week or less in 1979 than there had been in 1975, while during the same period the vacancy rate in the remaining hotels had plummeted from 26% to a mere 9%.

6 Of serious booklength studies, I know only two: Howard M. Bahr and Gerald R. Garrett, *Women Alone: The Disaffiliation of Urban Females,* Lexington Books, 1976; and *The Women Outside,* a study-in-progress by Stephanie Golden, soon to be published by St. Martin's Press.

7 Bahr and Garrett, *Women Alone,* Foreword by Theodore Caplow, p. xv.

8 Manhattan Bowery Corporation Report gives Census Bureau totals for 1976 of 5.1 million women over 65 living alone, and a 7.7 year edge in life expectancy of women over men (p. 13). Another study reports that while 75% of men 65 and over live with their spouses, only 38% of women do. Most women over 65 are widows. And over half of elderly widows live alone or with non-relatives. (Elizabeth W. Markson and Beth B. Hess, "Older Women in the City," *Signs,* Vol. 5, No. 3 Supplement, Spring 1980.)

9 Manhattan Bowery Corporation Report, pp. 30-33.

10 Hand, pp. 2-3, 10.

11 Bahr and Garrett, p. 130.

12 Bahr and Garrett, p. xv.

13 Nels Anderson, *The Hobo: The Sociology of the Homeless Man,* University of Chicago Press, 1923; Phoenix Edition, 1967, p. 137.

PREFACE

INTRODUCTION

What does it mean to be homeless? My home is not only a roof over my head. It is my anchor, a source of stability, a refuge from a world that is at times both stressful and alienating. When I go away it is the place I know I can return, in my thoughts when I am homesick, in reality when my travels are through. Because I am young, healthy and able to work I support this home. I have friends and family for other kinds of support. In this way I am privileged. If I became sick and incapacitated mentally or physically, if for some reason I could not support myself, who would take care of me? My friends and family might look out for me for awhile, but they have their own lives, and their own problems. What if my condition of joblessness or disability was serious and long lasting? The thought of being forced to rely on public charities is chilling. So it was with some apprehension that a few years ago I agreed to take a job teaching a recreational art class at the Shelter Care Center for Women in New York City. This center houses women who are, for a variety of reasons, without financial support or a place to live. My own worst fears about homelessness were heightened by this tangible manifestation of the reality for those who could not provide for themselves, but it was through my work there that I began to understand something about the lives of the women in the shelter and the prospects for all women in a society that does not adequately provide for the weak and the powerless.

The women at this residence were often in a crisis situation in their lives. Alcoholism, mental illness, evictions, family quarrels, mismanagement on welfare and lost or stolen funds had left them homeless. Some were older women suffering from physical illness and senility, a few were battered wives escaping from husbands and others were young girls running away from home or unable to find a job. They had in common an inability to deal adequately with severe personal problems.

I initially taught a class in painting and drawing, but when some interest developed in using an old instamatic camera, I was amazed at the response to the pictures the women took. Some had not seen photographs of themselves in twenty years. One woman peered intently at her image for a long time and asked over and over again if that was really her face. When I asked what she thought of it, she replied, "If that's me, I didn't know I looked that good." Using one broken camera and a few rolls of film, women began photographing everything in sight. This also opened up an opportunity for me to begin taking a few pictures of them. We all looked forward to seeing the results. We shared thoughts about the portrayal of character and the meaning of images. Our discussions were a relief from the boredom of institutional life and brought the women together to discover new interests and to relate to each other in new ways. The excitement generated in the classes was an inspiration for me to apply, then receive, a grant to teach an art and photography class at the shelter. I received funds for this purpose from the Metropolitan Museum in New York and the Joint Foundation Support, Inc. The women's work was exhibited at the Metropolitan Museum, Sirovich Community Center and The Queens Public Library.

My interest and closeness to the women continued to grow. Over and over I saw women enter and leave the shelter only to return weeks, months, or years later—each time a little worse for wear. I wondered what happened to them on the outside and why they didn't succeed. Many were deeply disturbed or alcoholic, but others, although they had acute personal problems, appeared to be "normal." What about their lives was different from mine? Was it possible that I too could find myself homeless? I began to see the workings of a social welfare system that ostensibly aims to lift people out of downtrodden paths, but all too often only succeeds in perpetuating and sometimes fostering their inability to help themselves.

Over a period of years I began taping interviews and photographing those women with whom I had developed a rapport. As my interest in the subject of homelessness grew, I began talking to the women I met on the streets of New York, then Boston and San Francisco.

There are many styles of homelessness. A few women are only temporarily without shelter. Others will experience crisis after crisis and will always end up on the streets. Some women receive welfare for varying lengths of time and live in "Single Room Occupancy" hotels. These S.R.O. hotels are for many just a short stop on the cycle back to the streets again.

Large cities are a mecca for people looking for excitement and adventure in otherwise desperate lives. For some, the city means hope and a blind stab at improving their circumstances.

Some get together just enough money to get on the bus and trust that things will work out once they arrive. It was with an adventurous spirit that one of the women I inter-

INTRODUCTION

viewed ran away from a nursing home in Illinois and came to New York. She brought hope for something better and a desire to see Macy's. She came to New York the same way that someone else might go on a vacation. Only, she had no funds, no place to stay, and no idea of what she was going to do when she got there. She preferred the freedom of testing her chances on the streets.

Shopping bag ladies are at the extreme end of the spectrum of homelessness. They are often older and suffer from the effects of the poverty and the social isolation of the middle-aged and elderly single woman. Many are mentally disabled. They have come to a point of total adaptation to living outside. Whether or not this is a "choice" is debatable, but it is true that once a woman has moved onto the streets it is very difficult to help her return to normalcy. Many women prefer independence to charity and social services.

Interviewing women on the streets was the most difficult part of my work. I looked for places where they stayed and found ways to approach them, but I found that some could not carry on coherent conversations, and were frightened and suspicious of me. If I could win their confidence, they were often delighted at the chance for company. It was often the first time anyone had listened to them in years. They seemed pleased to have the chance to express what they felt about their circumstances. Frequently, though, after establishing contact with a woman, explaining my project, and building a relationship with her over several days, she would refuse permission for me to take her photograph or tape our conversations. This reluctance was understandable. Often the women said they were ashamed and embarrassed by their situation, felt responsible for what they considered the failure in their lives, and did not feel they had any insights on the matter worth sharing.

The values of mainstream American life were not forgotten by these women. They felt drastically out of place, demoralized by their inability to establish homes, find work and belong. The cruel realities of their own lives conflicted with their desires to fulfill the stereotype of wife, mother, and daughter. To have no place in the world made them question their very right to be. Sensitive to the stares and curiosities of passersby, they nevertheless were rarely critical of a society that did not provide for them. For those I did get to know, it was always heartbreaking to find that there was little I could do to help other than to take them to the nearest shelter. Many times because of their past experiences in shelters, they refused to go. Time and again I would see women who had been homeless for only a short while fail to get meaningful assistance and gradually deteriorate.

In most large cities there are shelters for women run by public and private organizations. All homeless women are not in these shelters. There is not enough room for them. Few statistics exist about the exact numbers of homeless people in any city in America. But, every shelter providing services for these women reports that they must turn them away daily because there is no vacancy.

In many cities, shelters provide for the homeless on a restricted temporary basis. In Boston, for example, Harborlights and Rosie's Place serve free evening meals, but the bed space is limited and a woman is permitted to stay only several nights, then must find her own accommodations. After a certain amount of time has passed she can then repeat the cycle. This is to encourage women to move out of the shelter and to find a more suitable permanent place of residence. It insures that larger numbers of women will be serviced through the limited facilities available.

Other shelters also offer temporary housing for varying numbers of days. Women make the rounds, hoping to juggle the schedule of their days in and out among the particular shelters. Inevitably, though, the woman must spend a few days outdoors.

If there is a bed, and a woman can get into a residence, there are often further regulations with which she must comply. Many shelters are operated by religious organizations and require that applicants participate in services and religious indoctrination. Depending on a woman's inclination and need she may or may not wish to pay the price of cooperation. Still other shelters look for a "better grade" of client, women who they feel have some potential for reform and return to an acceptable place in society. They accept and work with women who are younger, have fewer years of hospitalization, some capacity to find a job and have spent less time on the streets.

In contrast, Rosie's Place in Boston prides itself on offering the women who come there problem-free services. Few, if any, personal questions are asked and a woman's request is all that is needed for her to obtain a bed. She may be receiving welfare, social security, have a job or even another place to live, but if she is first in line at Rosie's she gets a bed. All that is required of her is that she maintain a level of decorum in the dining hall and observe the six day cycle in and out. Alcohol, mental illness, and lack of cleanliness are tolerated within reason and there is an atmosphere of conviviality and friendliness amid the sadness and dire straits most of the women find themselves in. The largely volunteer staff is available to help with any problems of those who express some need, and there is an attempt made to connect women with social services and permanent housing. The Dwelling Place in New York City, and The House of Ruth in Washington are run along similar lines. These centers service the most needy and turn away no one if there is space available. But they have so few beds compared with the need.

Mary House in New York City is run by the Catholic Worker, an organization dedicated to helping the poor and to setting an example of decent Christian living. They concern themselves less with helping a woman move on to an independent life-style than allowing her to function as best as she can in a sheltered environment. Anyone may partake of the meals, clothing and medical care offered without question or requirements. Housing is offered on a more permanent basis, so there is only a small turnover and very few vacant beds.

Other shelters have more stringent requirements for admittance. In order to get into the Women's Shelter run by the city of New York, a woman must not have any funds available and must answer detailed questions about her past life and management. Alcohol and disruptive "acting out" is not allowed although this shelter is meant to service primarily alcoholic and mentally disturbed women. In order to receive services, a woman must go through the social work admittance interview, comply with many rules and regulations, allow her bags to be checked, take a compulsory shower, and submit to a medical exam and psychiatric interview. Many women refuse to go through these procedures which they perceive as invasive and humiliating.

Public Assistance often places many women in rooming houses or specially designated hotels. These rooms range from minimally acceptable to flagrantly violating all health codes. Heat may be sporadic, plumbing broken, paint peeling off the walls, locks left broken and hallways uncleaned and unguarded. Tenants are at the mercy of a landlord who is often absent, and whose main interest is in maintaining maximum profits at lowest expenditure. Without the advocates or the ability to find legal help, residents must endure the conditions of these rooms as they find them. Women are particularly vulnerable in this housing. They are often placed without supervision or protection among former inmates, addicts, mental patients, and transients with whom they must share bathroom and kitchen facilities. As usual the most defenseless are easy prey to the robberies and assaults that many times go unreported in these rooms. For these reasons some women feel they are safer outside on the streets.

Yet even these rooms, inadequate as they may be, are becoming more and more scarce. Landlords who once found it lucrative to fill their vacant hotels and rooming houses with referrals from welfare are now finding it even more profitable to convert these residences into housing for the middle class. Lured by the opportunity to make solid economic investments, these landlords were encouraged by city officials and block associations, who welcome this chance to clean up their neighborhoods. They perceived the deterioration of these neighborhoods as having been brought on by the influx of large numbers of ex-mental patients and welfare recipients who filled the hotels. This has resulted in the displacement of the urban poor who were managing on subsistence levels in the rooms that are now being converted to expensive apartments or torn down altogether. Dislocation of residents already at the bottom of the economic bracket has meant an increase in the numbers of people who could make no other "adjustment" but to turn to living on the streets. Urban renewal efforts impact significantly on the lives of the most disadvantaged. Cities are faced with the Hobson's choice of developing neighborhoods or displacing the poor.

Those lucky enough to find decent housing in a hotel must then cope with the difficulties of making do with the small amount of money they have leftover after paying the rent. If there are no cooking facilities, and this is not unusual, a woman must find a way to stretch her budget to cover eating in restaurants, carfare and all other necessities. Providing all goes smoothly she may be able to get by. Too often, checks don't show up, arguments develop with the landlord over her room, emotional problems intensify, or she is unable to budget her check and runs out of money.

Because these women receive no consistent support in managing their lives the recidivism rate to the shelters is very high. Women return again and again, each time a little worse off. In San Francisco, Boston and

New York the brutal reality remains that for the large numbers of women on the streets who need help and a place to stay, there are too few public shelters to accommodate them, and nowhere for them to find the follow-up and ongoing care that would help them maintain themselves off the streets.

I wondered about the families of the women I met in the streets. Where were their relatives, husbands, children and parents who might be expected to help? Many women on the streets have no families. Through illness, death, divorce, family hostilities and resentments, all contact with close relatives has been lost. Familial ties have been broken by long separations in hospitals or by the great distances that easy mobility in this country allows. There is no community of relatives or friends to rely on. Alone and isolated in the world, these women have no one to turn to.

Yet I also met homeless women who had families and even a certain amount of contact with them. In some cases the family was well aware of the plight of the relative, but they were already so overburdened with struggles to maintain a degree of economic and mental stability themselves that there was simply no strength or money to provide for another member who could not carry her full share. But it is not poverty alone that causes a family to cast out a member. Some of the women I met, although not the majority, were from middle-class families. Alcoholism and mental illness place tremendous strains on any family. Often after years of struggling to sustain and support an ill person, relatives have given up. For their own survival they come to the conclusion that they have done all that is humanly possible, and, in order to preserve the stability they have salvaged, they stop giving energy and resources to a relative who cannot contribute or will not take care of herself. Other women choose to have no contact with their relatives because they do not want to be a burden to them.

Deinstitutionalization, sometimes referred to as 'dumping' has often been cited as the reason for the increasingly large numbers of homeless women and men seen on our city streets. More than fifteen years ago, the government undertook to change the mental health system by releasing long-term patients to halfway houses and treatment in outpatient community centers. Several factors were instrumental in bringing this change about: recognition that long years in psychiatric hospitals rarely benefited anyone and in fact harmed some, the introduction of new psychoactive drugs, and finally the increasing rise in cost of patient care in large institutions. The initial objective of emptying mental hospitals, although guided more by economic factors than humane intent, was founded in progressive ideas. Patients who had formerly been consigned to long stays in a mental hospital were now given short-term treatment and turned back into the community. Once considered manageable only within the confines of an institution, they could now be maintained with drugs as outpatients. Theoretically, there was to be a discharge plan for every individual. Unfortunately for those without families or other support this usually consisted of carfare to the nearest welfare office.

These policies contributed to a situation of chaos and neglect in the management of ex-patients. Only a few of the proposed system of small mental health centers ever materialized to meet the needs of the large numbers being turned out from the hospitals —medication clutched in hand. The worsening economy reduced available funding. Neighborhoods objected to mental patients housed in their midst and the results of drugs, or other types of therapy for the severely mentally ill proved uncertain at best.

However, these policies were successful in reducing the inpatient population of large mental hospitals. Between 1955 and 1975 there was a 65 percent decrease in the census of resident patients in state mental hospitals. It has also meant a growing proportion of readmissions into those same hospitals and an influx of patients using the services of emergency rooms, shelters and clinics by the many who fail to make it on the outside.

Public outrage and problems resulting from this has been well documented. Worse though, for thousands of people released to a nonexistent system of community aftercare, this policy has meant a battle to survive a transition from the "back wards to the back alleys." Unable to cope with the anxieties and stress of competing for jobs and housing, many of these former patients drift about unprotected and unprovided for on the streets. Although sent to welfare or the social security offices, they often become "lost," only to turn up in emergency rooms or to be seen sleeping in public places.

This is not to imply that all homeless women on the streets or in the shelters have been in and out of mental hospitals. While it is true that many have spent years in hospitals and are the victims of deinstitutionalization, others have managed to avoid hospitalization, because of the more stringent requirements for admittance. The unusual and extreme stress of living on the streets tends to exacerbate emotional disturbances, and most of the women I met had great difficulties in effectively dealing with their problems, yet not all of them could be described as mentally ill.

In exploring how women survived on the streets, I spent many hours sitting in train stations, meeting and talking with women who made these places their homes. There is a kind of stupor that one can fall into sitting over long periods with no place to go. In one large station there are no windows. Time passes eerily under the perpetual fluorescent lighting. Some women spend entire days there. In that atmosphere I became aware I would easily lose track of time as the hours slipped by, one undifferentiated from the next. I found myself passively sinking into an immobilized daze, talking to someone or staring off blankly into space as the day passed from evening to night to morning. It was difficult at times to find the energy to get up and leave.

Finding a place to sleep is a major problem for the women. Waiting rooms, subways, and all-night restaurants can at times provide a temporary safe shelter from men as well as a resting place, but there is always the inevitable moment when she is asked to move along. In train stations, police make hourly rounds to shake the shoulders of anyone who falls asleep and to give a solid whack to the soles of the feet of those they have had to remind one time too many. Some women are asked to leave, but those deemed presentable are allowed to stay as long as they can keep their eyes open. Rarely can a woman get a full night's sleep in any of these places. Because of the many difficul-

ties she encounters in even trying to get rest she is forced to live in a perpetual state of extreme weariness and exhaustion. We see them sleeping in public so often because it is better to wait until daylight to find a doorway or a park bench that might be more conspicuous but is at least safe.

Sleep deprivation disorients and confuses even those with the strongest of minds. When this is combined with poor nutrition, lack of shelter, constant exposure to the elements, and physical and mental infirmities, many women spend their days in a continual fog of fatigue. Never getting a chance to lie down also causes circulatory problems. Long hours spent walking or sitting means they are especially prone to swollen, ulcerated legs. Once ulcers start, repeated irritation, poor treatment, and lack of cleanliness makes them all the more difficult to cure. Under these circumstances the women struggle to maintain themselves as best they can.

Train stations have the advantage of accessible ladies rooms. Whole communities live in some of them. The women in the waiting rooms stay short distances apart from each other. They usually wait until after rush hour to take seats, and then sit upright attempting to sleep or stay awake—inconspicuous travelers with their bags, until one notices the swollen legs and flimsy house slippers on even cold winter days.

These stations provide many of the amenities of a hotel—a roof over one's head, warmth, sinks for washing, and the anonymous crowds in which to lose oneself and join in the spectacle of watching other passersby. The women wait for a train that doesn't come, wait to get warm, wait for the police to kick them out and wait for the day

to pass. In one station there is a mass exodus to the ladies room after eleven P.M. when the attendant goes off duty. The euphemism of "rest room" is an apt description for a place where a woman can quite literally find rest. Depending on the presence or good will of an attendant, women may at times use these rooms to find a few hours of uninterrupted sleep. They will be reasonably protected by each other's presence until the police come as they do most every night to shoo them out around three or four A.M.

In one station on cold nights there is a waiting line to get to the blow-dryer to warm frozen hands, and to dry hair or clothing. An old lady without a coat stands under the blower. She tries to push the button and to fall asleep at the same time. Succeeding for seconds at a time she begins crumpling to the floor and jolts herself awake to press the button again. The incessant whirring of the dryer is added to the muffled snoring in one corner, the noise of running water of those washing at the sinks, and the self-contained dialogues of two or three women carrying on boozy conversations with themselves. Occasional shouting matches break out among women accusing each other of stealing or whoring or "Not being fit to sleep in a rat pack!" The old lady finds herself a trash bin to sit on and gradually the silences grow loud between her wakings to press the button.

Most of the women seem to be in their own worlds, talking to themselves or just sleeping quietly in corners. Few are very friendly with each other or anyone else. They are wary of contact with people and find that they are safer and less bothered if they keep to themselves. At the station it is important to keep as low a profile as possible in order to blend in with the travelers and not get asked to leave.

There is a small group who share a kind of camaraderie, saying hello to one another, pairing up in friendships to walk around the station, checking out the coin boxes of the telephones and sitting together in the waiting room. These are the women I have been talking to and getting to know.

Sonia, a Spanish woman with brown eyes and a pretty face has befriended me. She says she has lived in the station for three years and knows everyone who lives there and works there. Sonia panhandles enough to support four lockers for all her possessions. Most of what she has is clothing and a few treasured items, including a mirror, a tiny statue, and magazines. Supporting these lockers consumes much of her time as they have to be "fed" every twenty-four hours. On the occasions when she can't get the money together, and the twenty-four hours are up, her possessions are taken out of the lockers and put in storage at a daily rate. As the days pass and she is unable to get the money, the bill mounts up and she periodically loses everything—only to acquire new things and begin the process all over again. This is a common pattern for many women.

When I tell Sonia I am doing research about homelessness she immediately begins to tell me bits of gossip about all the women around us. One woman she says is really crazy. Mary and Beatrice are her friends. The old lady by the blower lives in an SRO hotel near the station, but she is senile and comes nearly every night to sleep and keep warm.

A black woman in a salmon sweater, who like several others has a huge amount of gear, sets herself up in one of the toilet stalls on the floor. It is almost like taking a room in a hotel. They put up newspapers to cover the bottom of the stall door for privacy. Sonia tells me that one woman, who eyes us very suspiciously is really a prostitute in the South Bronx. She gives all her money to a pimp. She comes here every night because she has nowhere else to go. I remark on the sadness of her situation, but Sonia clearly disapproves and has little sympathy. Later, as the night wears on, I see prostitutes bring men down to the toilet stalls. If all these "rooms" are taken they leave to return later. There are stories about the men who find their way down there, beat up various women, and steal their bags. Beatrice says that the police use less than gentle treatment in clearing out the room in the morning.

It is Elsie who cleans up. She busily washes the mirrors, sweeps the floors, and empties the trash bin, all the while humming softly to herself. Sonia doesn't like Elsie. She says she steals from the other women while they're asleep. The paid attendant told me that the women who sleep there always leave it neat and in order. In the mornings, when she comes to work, she rarely has to pick up after anyone.

Sandra Rollins wanders in late each night to wash up at the sinks. At the women's shelter, through the classes I taught, I had come to know her well. She was always friendly and sociable. I last heard that she had been placed in a hotel, but Sandra has a history of mismanagement on welfare. In the hotels, when isolation becomes overwhelming, when she overspends her rent money, or gets mugged, or her checks simply do not arrive, Sandra packs what she has and takes to the streets.

As we pass I look directly at her to say hello, but she stares blankly and seems to see right through me. I hesitate to remind her of our acquaintance. I'd seen another woman from the shelter whom I recognized and said hello to when she asked me for a quarter. But it was the wrong thing to do. As I gave her the quarter and said, "Aren't you Martha K.?" she suddenly leaped up and came after me screaming the loudest sound I've ever heard. I ran for my life. I now pass quickly by her in the station where I often see her giggling, shouting, walking about in a daze or sleeping. I do not know if she recognizes me or remembers anything.

Sonia and Mary and Beatrice commiserate about "these poor unfortunate women that live down here and have nowhere to go." Shaking their heads sadly they tell me, "Something really ought to be done about it." "They're called shopping bag ladies," the three of them tell me. "Some of these women have checks and lots of money in those bags." They, themselves help to perpetuate the famous myth about shopping bag ladies really having a lot of money. I ask this group for facts, but nobody can tell me anything concrete. Sonia merely nods her head knowingly and assures me that it is true. Mary and Beatrice agree.* Mary then goes on to say that, "You know it's because they're closing down the mental hospitals that you have so many of these unfortunates down here."

Mary and Beatrice sleep nearly every night in the station and Sonia says she has lived there for years. None of them are on welfare, get social security checks, or have anywhere else to go. They each carry around a collection of bags with all their possessions, yet none of them considers herself a "shopping bag lady," (a term which they regard as derogatory) or, for that matter, particularly homeless. They explain that they are simply temporarily without funds and down and out on their luck—even if it has been for years.

For some of the women I met I had a small hope that through luck or endurance they would eventually create a reasonable life for themselves. These were the women who had left within them resources of inner strength, emotional stability, and enough will to fight for the minimal scraps of help offered here and there by individuals and social agencies. But the lives of most of the women have been lost. Profound and irrevocable maltreatment and deprivation at every turn has denied them the psychological and material necessities of a life outside an institution, or off the streets. The long term intensive help that might have saved them was rarely available. I was forced to accept the reality of human fate in which none of us can save the other, and yet in which we must never cease to make every effort to give help so that another can save herself.

To be without a home is to be invisible. Because the needs and the lives of the homeless are unacknowledged, they remain in this sense unseen. By revealing the hidden world of those who are without even the rudimentary protection of shelter, I have raised questions about the prospects for those who cannot provide for themselves in this society. Opening our eyes to their experiences illuminates all our lives.

—*Ann Marie Rousseau*

*Newspaper articles and television programs have focused on stories about homeless women with large amounts of money and uncashed checks found in their bags. While it is true that there have been certain well-publicized cases of women with extensive funds available in bank accounts, for the most part the women on the streets have very little, if any, money. They at times have the money from welfare and S.S.I. checks that they are using to subsist on, but find inadequate to pay for a room or an apartment. Most of the women are not receiving any checks and have only the money they can get from asking strangers or none at all. The names in this book have been changed.

Photograph on page 15 of author
by Deborah Richardson

INTRODUCTION

A DAY IN THE LIFE OF HELEN TRENTON

A DAY IN THE LIFE OF HELEN TRENTON

HELEN TRENTON

In nearly every city there is somewhere to get free food. In New York this means going to the bread line at St. Francis's at five in the morning. In Boston it might be waiting until five in the evening to go to Rosie's Place for dinner. In San Francisco, at St. Anthony's Dining Hall, men start lining up around ten in the morning for lunch at noon while women and the infirm are able to go to the head of the line and immediately sit down at a table. For many of these people the focus of their entire day is finding food.

Helen Trenton tries to get to St. Anthony's most mornings. I watch her eat the nourishing but none too appetizing scrambled eggs, creamed vegetables, hot dogs, white bread, mashed potatoes, donuts and the surprisingly good coffee that is served. Helen has been talking about the tiny dots on her arms and neck, the pain she is having behind her ears, and the pain she feels in her hands that is bothering her so much that she can hardly hold onto her spoon. She has a neatly wrapped bundle parked under her chair and I wonder if she too lives in an S.R.O. hotel like Francis who I had met earlier. When I suggest that she check her mattress for bugs as a possible cause of the red dots, she says, "No that couldn't be it because I'm not staying anywhere." We chat for awhile longer discussing the food, her pains and the project that I am working on. I tell her I am writing a book on homeless women and want to record what she has to say about her life. We agree to spend the day together and then carefully wrap up our leftovers and go out to the street.

Helen's first stop is usually the county library where she likes to spend most afternoons. It is not far from St. Anthony's and so we stroll over to it through a cool December day that is threatening rain. At the library we take the elevator up to the second floor reading room and Helen picks out a table and we sit down. She is reasonably neat and quiet and no one bothers her as she reads her daily paper. She does not usually read a current one, preferring instead a paper she has found along the way.

In order to read she puts on a pair of men's horn-rimmed glasses that she has found on the street. As the hours go by she reads every single article, from front to back, the real estate section, the obituaries and all of the want ads. When she is finished it is late in the afternoon and she decides that she should be getting over to the hospital emergency room to have her spots checked. As we are waiting for the elevator, Helen is delighted to find both a large cigarette butt and a wholly unsmoked cigarette lying on the floor. She immediately sits down on the floor to enjoy this unexpected bonus, generously offering to share them with me but, as I don't smoke, I decline.

We talk and she tells me that before this morning's meal at St. Anthony's she had not eaten for two days. She has had "only two scotches" with a friend and afterwards lost track of both the time and her consciousness. When she woke up, she found blood on her scalp and her false teeth missing. She told me that after she felt better, she walked over to St. Anthony's.

People stare at us sitting on the floor but Helen seems not to notice them. She enjoys her cigarette but winces every so often at the pain that continues to cramp her thin hands. It is only three o'clock but it seems like we have been sitting endlessly all day. I grow bored and uncomfortable. Helen scratches at the red marks on her arms and neck. As she scratches, she pulls off little flakes and flicks them to the floor. One of them crawls away. Maybe she has scabies. I have the creeps. Soon I am scratching and picking at my hair too.

Finally we are off to the hospital emergency room where Helen often spends the night in a waiting room chair. Tonight is different because she has a medical problem to be looked at. As we are waiting for the bus, I am wondering how she will pay for it since I know that she doesn't have much money. But Helen very simply and sweetly asks the driver if he will accept her only nickle and he agrees to let her ride for that. She is not able, however, to glide so smoothly through the bureaucracy of the emergency room. A receptionist has a form before him which must be filled out and he asks many routine questions including her place of residence. "I exist on Catholic Charities," Helen replies. But the man insists he must have an address to put on the form. Instead of making one up Helen fumes and stamps and shouts and says loudly, "I don't stay anywhere!" "Employed?" is the next question but Helen is really aggravated now and refuses to answer anything more. The young man's temper is aroused too, and at the end of an angry exchange he says that she must sit down until she is ready to answer all of the questions. We go off to sit in a corner and I suspect that her name has not been put on the waiting list. But after an hour she is called to be seen by a doctor. Another hour goes by of endless sitting and waiting and still she has

A DAY IN THE LIFE OF HELEN TRENTON

not returned. Already a man that was brought in unconscious on a stretcher has walked out looking healthy and even smiling. More people filter in and out of the emergency room; most are black and poor. The police bring in a man in handcuffs.

I finally ask the receptionist what has happened to Helen and I am sent back to find her. In a tiny room, a young student doctor is taking care of her. Helen has a thick file at this hospital. Apparently she comes here whenever she needs a shower or when she wants to be deloused. The doctor says that the cramping in her hands is caused by an insecticide that she applied to her skin more than three weeks ago but never washed off. He cleans her hands but she is still infected with the parasites and has to be deloused. A nurse gives her a bottle of lotion and tells her to take a shower with it. They also find some clothes for her and ask her to throw away what she is wearing and everything that she is carrying. She does this willingly, going through her possessions and pulling out her papers and a few other articles and putting them into a bag that the nurse has provided. She seems to know the routine and does everything rather compliantly but she is very concerned that they find her a hat. Her hair is very long and tangled. She does not comb it and appears self-conscious about this. The best they can find is a white linen towel to serve as a scarf.

After her shower a social worker asks her about eight times in five different ways if she would like to go to an adult care home. The worker promises to investigate whether or not Helen is eligible for SSI payments but says she'll have to wait until the morning. For the time being, everyone tries to get Helen into some temporary housing. She seems to miss the question each time, saying that she doesn't want to be locked up anywhere. She has a great fear of being imprisoned and is convinced that the social worker is really trying to put her into an institution. The worker patiently tries to explain that they aren't allowed to lock anybody up but they do try to keep an eye out for people. Again they say that in the morning they will try to reinstate her SSI payments. Helen is certain that she will not get any checks. She is not very clear about why, but she has had too many problems before and has given up trying. The home that they are proposing sending her to is in a bad neighborhood, and so she adamantly refuses to go. She would prefer instead to fend for herself in her usual manner. Many nights she simply stays in a waiting room chair and she wants to stay there tonight. She finds it comfortable enough and it is better than riding the buses around which she thinks is her only other option. Out of frustration they agree to let her stay in the emergency unit for one night.

I suspect that because of my presence, the doctor and social worker have taken more than the usual interest in Helen. They gave us both permission to sleep in the waiting room, going against hospital policy, and they kindly gave us some baloney and cheese sandwiches. We went off to sit in the chairs and Helen made herself at home. I am not fond of baloney and cheese, but I devoured the sandwiches just as eagerly as Helen. Time clicked away through the night. The staff told us that they would notify the security guards of our presence, but toward morning we are asked to leave. Normally, Helen says, she would get on a bus and ride for awhile, but because they have let her stay longer this time, she decides to go to the main lobby and wait for the morning shift to come on duty. There we find more comfortable seats and settle down. Helen is waiting for a meeting later with the social worker who is going to find her a room. After more time has passed I get up to leave because I have an appointment later that day and I want to get some warmer clothes. I make an arrangement to meet Helen later.

In researching her case the social worker discovered that Helen was due a backlog of Social Security checks amounting to $1125. A year and a half ago she had been placed on disability in a Board and Care Home but had disappeared before she collected any money. They listed her whereabouts as "unknown." The social worker sent her to the SSI office to collect enough of her check to last for the rest of the week and tried to find a conservator to help her manage the rest. At the office however, due to a bureaucratic mistake, Helen was given the entire $1125. She then went to cash the check and told the man at the counter that it was for $125. He saw that she was disoriented and confused so he called the social worker to find out what should be done. They arranged to give her only fifty dollars and then sent her to a hotel where I was to meet her. She was given the address and clear directions on how to get there. They said that she seemed to understand and had assured them that she could find her way easily because she was very familiar with all the bus routes. Unfortunately she never made it. Perhaps she thought that the hotel was actually an institution. I don't know. What I do know is that after

A DAY IN THE LIFE OF HELEN TRENTON

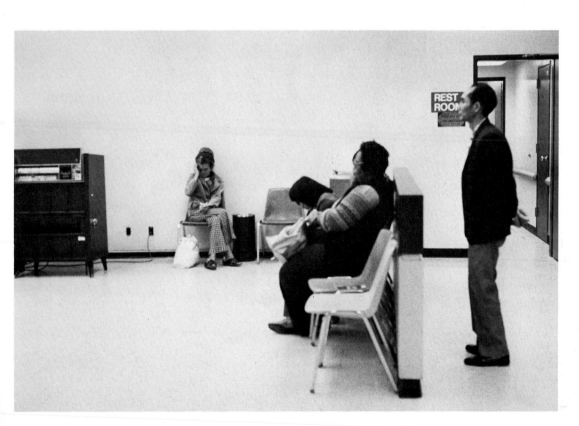

picking up her fifty dollars she once again disappeared onto the streets, her whereabouts "unknown."

—A.M.R.

HELEN

I haven't been living very well. You see there are places that are opened all night, restaurants that are opened. In other words in some of these places like on 23rd and Bryant, they let you put your head down and sleep for fifteen, twenty minutes, even before you eat or after you eat. But mostly they don't.

I sleep sitting up because the doctors advise it. I guess it's kind of a new program. I've gotten used to it but I get so tired. The first week you go through that and you don't know how long you're going to stay awake. You walk around like you're drunk. You're in a haze. You just ain't up to the highway patrol. Once when I was walking across the street, looking for this place for breakfast at five o'clock in the morning, I stumbled because I was so tired, overtired. I had been walking two or three days and I guess they wanted to pick me up.

Most days after I eat breakfast at St. Anthony's I probably go to the library. I read the paper, something like that. I picked up some glasses on the street because my eyes are bad. It's been so long since I've been able to focus on something accurately. On anything as far as the reading goes.

Let's see, what is today? Wednesday? The library's open till nine. In other words there is heat there. But mostly I just stay long enough to read the paper, then go downstairs to freshen up, to use the bathrooms.

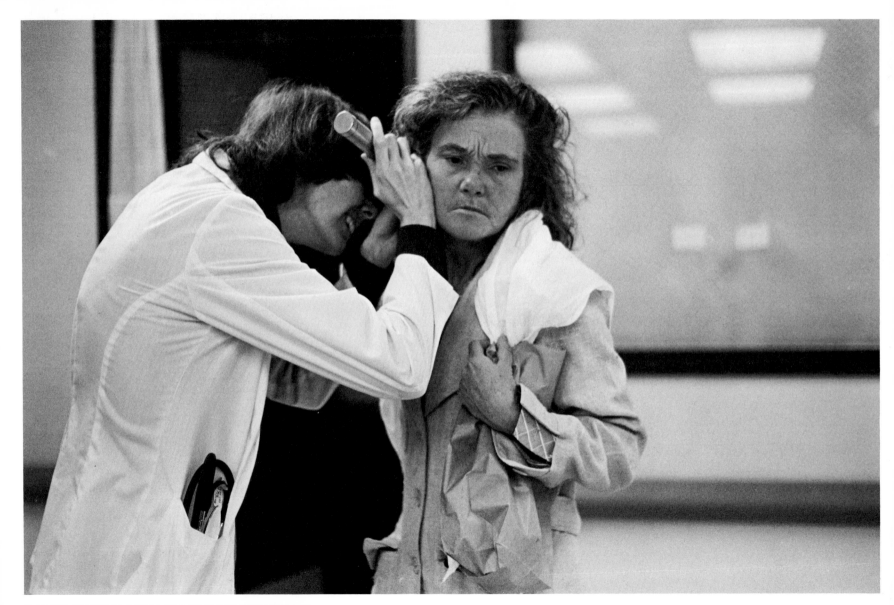

A DAY IN THE LIFE OF HELEN TRENTON

Bathrooms are hard to find. If I'm lucky I'll make it to Zims. They'll let you in. But I don't like to lean on them. At McDonald's they have a pretty good rest room but then again somebody's always eyeing you. They think you're taking advantage of them.

I sometimes come out to the hospital and change and wash up almost every day, downstairs in emergency. You know, wash up, comb my hair, change clothes. I stay in the waiting room and sleep nights, but at three o'clock in the morning you're ordered out with everybody else. Then I get on the bus until the morning when the front doors open and the seven o'clock crew comes in. I ride the number 25 and transfer to the number 22. I go over to the Filmore area, get off and come back. It's warm on the bus. Sometimes the driver will take a nickle, depends on how familiar I ask. But then sometimes they'll tell you to get off even if it's raining outside. Then I walk, but I can't take much more of it because my legs are starting to bother me. My ankles are swollen and I've been pretty exhausted.

I saw my daughter about three months ago but she was pretty broke and so was I. See, when I was getting my checks I used to always bring them groceries. I'd stop off at the day old shop and get five or six loaves of the best bread that there is. Just like I was some kind of millionaire I picked out the wheat bread. It was really good. I'd leave it on her doorstep if she wasn't home.

When my girls were put in foster care I went to a place for adults over in the shopping district. It was an adult care home and I fol-

A DAY IN THE LIFE OF HELEN TRENTON

lowed a handicap program at the Goodwill. They knew they had me the minute they got me into that program. Throwing me into a home so I lost my independence and what marriages there were. It was a drain on the pocketbook. I couldn't get anything for a cent. In those places you have to expect to see no evil, hear no evil, and speak no evil. The mind can only take it for so long. I didn't sleep the whole year I was in there. Don't ask me why. The sleeping mechanism was just damaged. These old birds out on the streets aren't there because of economic reasons. Chances are they couldn't sleep if they had a good comfortable bed.

I left the home when I became ill. See I went out with a group to Chinatown and I didn't mind going but I was running a fever. I had a cold and those rooms weren't very warm. I was in that place a year and I didn't take my coat off for the whole year, from early morning to late at night. Well, the party got ahead of me. I was dizzy for a moment then I turned around and they were gone. I got on a bus and came out here to the hospital. I just never went back. They called from there and said if you're unhappy don't come back. I didn't face any of the situation at the time.

Once I was living at a hotel over on Post or Sutter. I forget. But the rooms weren't very good. Then they out and out told me that they make more profit out of prostitutes. That's the way it is in these hotels. That's what these people are facing. In other words if there's a big convention in town you have to be out on the streets maybe for the week-

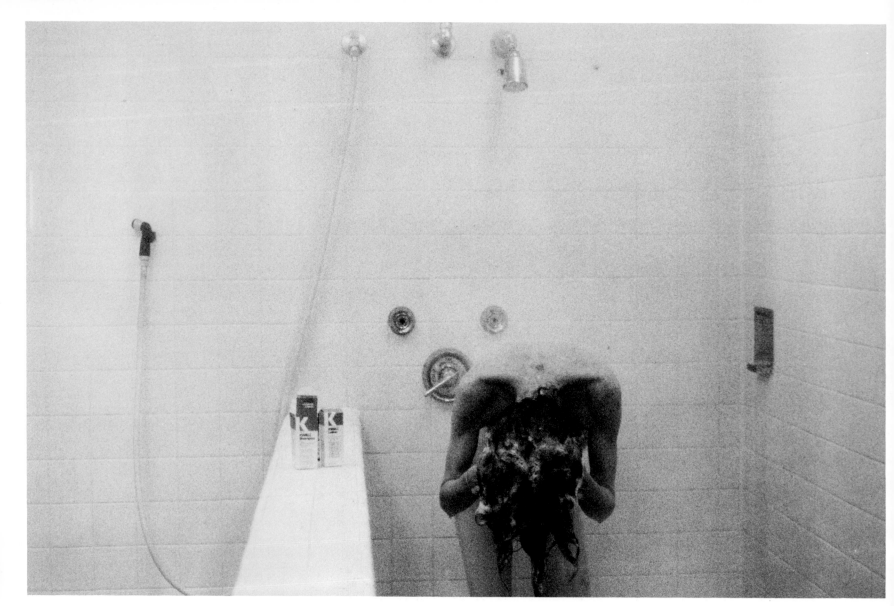

A DAY IN THE LIFE OF HELEN TRENTON

end. It's been a year and a half now and I'm still living outside on the streets.

I don't know what I'll do now. Try to get work I guess. Certainly not getting anywhere sitting on my ass, pardon me, with the welfare and social security. What work? At my age I haven't the vaguest. I'm almost fifty and that isn't easy after twenty-five years of not working, raising a family. I'll try to collect unemployment insurance, of course I haven't worked.

Very interesting situation. Maybe I'll come back to the hospital. I just know the area around here. Like a cat or a dog I come back, rotate toward it when I'm uncertain, I guess.

RAYNA LANDRY

RAYNA LANDRY

I'm not in the habit of talking. Maybe I'm talking too much but you have to explain yourself. You see, in the hotel I was in they gave us money but we should have had protection too. Most of the people in that hotel were like the worst ones in Rockland State Hospital. I found out the other day that they've only got 1000 beds up there but we've got 15,000 of those people let out down here in New York City on us. The sane just aren't safe on the subways or in the houses with them because they are stealing off nice people that are getting checks. We're in danger.

Alright dear, you know that they don't act like us but you know that I'm more reasonable about this than most because I've been on the streets longer than anybody. In twelve years I've learned and watched. I understand some of these people from the hospitals. I know the nice ones, the ones you don't have to worry about. But I'm afraid. Some doctors are very poor judges and they let all kinds come down here to the hotels besides the drug addicts and alcoholics.

In my hotel they even had professional crooks. Alright I forgot to lock my door when I went to the toilet, but I was living with thieves so much I forgot. Once on the elevator, two crooks followed me and robbed me. They robbed me in my room too. I was sleeping and somebody came in and feeled me up and I chased him out. I don't know how he got in. He was a mental defective from cancer and he's all cut up. He and his girlfriend were doing a lot of holdups. They were both like this. They'd come inside and turn your mattress over. When they drink

RAYNA LANDRY

they look for money. Professional crooks right in the hotel! He's still there and they're still getting away with it.

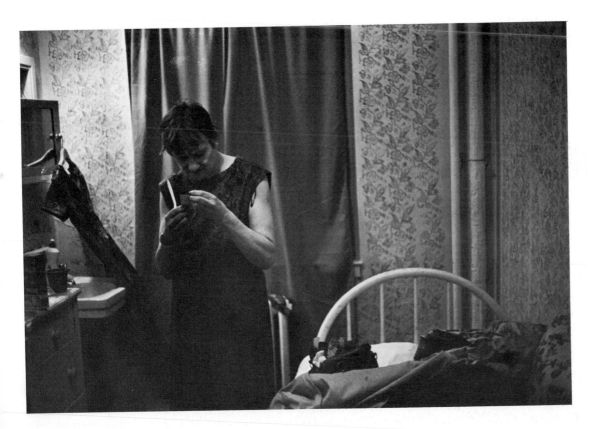

I only went to the seventh grade. I wasn't alert. I was very dumb. I still don't know a lot of things, even today. Nobody would help me but my daddy. He tried to help me but he didn't know how. The second year that they were going to keep me in the seventh grade I had a bad sickness, spinal meningitis, and I was taken out of school. I never went back. After that, when I was fifteen, I worked in a factory making cigars. I used to roll them up like cigarettes.

My problem was my name but you can change your name anytime you want. My first name was Mary, my second was Rayna, but Mary made me have trouble. I hated it so I'm using Rayna for now and it's been awhile. My name shouldn't have been Mary. I should have been Shirley. If I was a boy I should have been Lou. See, we're given the wrong names and our names fix us.

I always worked. I worked for a rich lady up on 77th Street. I was cooking for company and everything. You know, eight and nine tables. She had parties twice a week. She paid me but they didn't want to know about signatures or tax. Nothing. They tell you that they don't remember so they don't have the tax to write up and the paper work. See? But I like housework. Well that's all I could do in them days. It was the depression dear, and we'd get three, five dollars a week. A doctor I know gave me ten dollars a month to babysit his kids but in them days we took the job. Of course I never could get

RAYNA LANDRY

a job after my husband died. I would never even have gotten on charity if I could have gotten in a good home. I would have stayed in housework, but carrying all the papers around all the time makes me sick.

In '67 I went to the Pioneer Hotel when my check didn't come in. The girls there were all dead from drinking. It was a terrible place but we didn't have to take showers and get checked like now. We'd sleep and in the morning we had to bring all our stuff and check out until night. We took our shopping bags with us.

The last hotel I stayed in was a thievy hotel. You could get robbed as soon as you went out. I had no running water, no locks in the bathroom, people could even grab you from behind. There were murders there, thievery, killing, dope fiends. I was scared. I heard screaming there at night, a woman. I don't know why. That place was getting bad but you get so used to it. As soon as I go out at night I have fear because I don't know who's in back of me. I've been robbed so much.

When I run out of money I beg a coffee and a bagel and live off that, but I don't like to beg much and I hope I don't have to do that again. I wouldn't even chisel a cigarette. When I worked I didn't like anybody to do this either, but then we all lose our pride. When you lose your pride it's the worst thing. Nobody thinks you're any good. When I want a quarter, I need and I get it, but I also tell all those people on the street that I might never see them again. They're sure the lucky ones because they have their pride left.

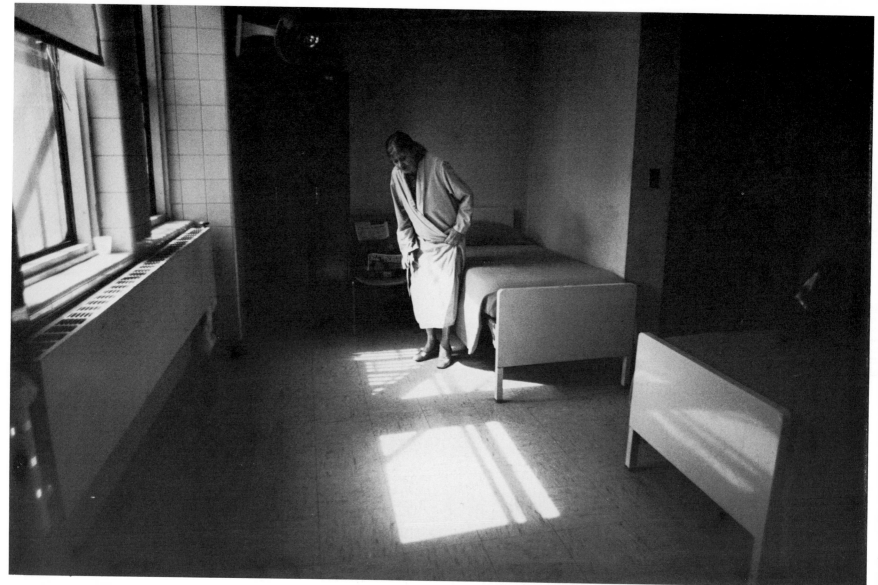

RAYNA LANDRY

Before I came to the Shelter? Oh, starving. I didn't eat for weeks. I paid the rent at that hotel with one check and they robbed my eating money. So, I had a room, a tiny room, and I stayed there. It was cold. They didn't have steam, nothing, because the furnace broke. It's a cold winter. I just stayed in bed all day. After awhile I was too weak to go out or even to bathe. When the others found me they put me right up in the Shelter. "You'll be alright, we'll feed you," they told me.

I'm really grateful to them. Believe me if I had a lot of money I'd give it to them.

DIFFICULTIES

HATTIE MAE BARNES

Today I'm going to find an apartment. I don't know where I'm going. I'm just going around looking for a room. The thing is I don't have any money. Now if I can get my check at the center, maybe I can find a place. They sent me a letter that said they were cutting out this and cutting out that. I used to get $235 a month for rent and food but when I was living with the lady on Edwards Street, they cut it down to $135. I'd like to go back to work again but I've lost so much time. I haven't worked for a year. I can't stand to be idle that much. I know it keeps you young and beautiful when you work. It gives you something to do. It gives you peace of mind.

I was from Virginia and I was there until 1929. I came to New York during the Wall Street crash. I came here because I could make more money than I could in Virginia at the time. Here they were paying four dollars a day, then they got down to two dollars a day. I was doing domestic work. I was a cook for a private family in New York and then I was cooking in restaurants and hotels in the mountains. I was a chef until 1961. Then I retired because my sister was sick and I had to leave New Hampshire. I worked many camps down the line. I think I liked the mountains better because it was cooler and I liked the trees and the birds and the greens.

I was eighteen when I got married. I stayed married a couple of years and then I went off. We agreed to separate. I was about twenty. He died in March 1928 of walking pneumonia. I never had any kids and I never married again. I had my sister bring her children up north to Brooklyn when I was living there because my brother-in-law was sick. My sister got sick and passed away in 1961 and my brother in 1963. My other brother got lost. I don't know where he is. He just left home when he was fourteen, so I have no one now. I'm all alone.

When I became sixty-two I got social security and disability but my checks got mangled up because I was staying one place and then I moved. That's when I had the accident. My ankle got fractured, something in it got broken. I didn't like the place I lived in after that so well. It was noisy and you couldn't get to sleep. But I didn't leave. I was dispossessed because I came back from the hospital sick and I wasn't able to keep up. My niece lived up the block so she came down and helped me as much as she could to put my things in storage. I guess they must still be there. I hope. This July 31st it will be a year since I put them there.

When I had to leave I went to my friends' house. My friends didn't have a lot of room because they are a family and they had to put some of their stuff away to let me stay there. Then I went to stay with a lady on Edwards Street and the checks got all mixed up. When I changed the address the girl I was staying with got all scared because she was on welfare and I wasn't paying no rent. She really didn't have enough room anyway. I had to sleep in the little girl's room, so I went back to the family for awhile. I wouldn't go to my niece because I knew how they were situated. I don't want to make it uncomfortable for anyone.

Finally I went down to welfare and tried to get on. It took me two days, staying there all day. I said, "What can I do? Is there any place I could go because I'm crippled and I'm walking on a stick?" I had no money or work. So they said there's a shelter on Lafayette Street and that's how I got here. I heard that there were all kinds of people in the shelters. Women lovers and this and that but I don't see nothing wrong with this place. I have no fault to find.

LESLIE WILLOW

Originally I'm from Florida. My parents were divorced so I had a series of stepmothers and it was better to be away after that. I stayed with my father. We really didn't have a choice. My mother had left. I wasn't young when they divorced. I was about 13 or 14. I later went to Florida State College. I got a degree in English and Psychology. After I graduated I went to Baltimore for three years, to work with Westinghouse. I had two different jobs. Eventually I was transferred. They put in a sound system among all the Westinghouse plants, so they put me in charge of planning the programs. They had music and so many times a day we'd play speeches from the officers, vice-president, talking to the people, news broadcasts during rest periods and lunch. Eventually it got to be the same old routine. So I left to take a job at a planned parenthood clinic, and from there I went back to school.

It was during this time that I was being psychoanalyzed. Real psychoanalysis. Five times a week. I was lucky I had a wonderful doctor. Not just a typical straight Freudian where you sit there passively and listen. It saved my life. It was the most important thing I ever did because I'm sure it saved me from being in a mental hospital. I never spent a day in a mental hospital and I'm sure I would have if I didn't have it. I don't mean it solved my problems or anything like that. I was in my 20's then and I was getting these panic feelings occasionally. It was like having a glass wall around me. I cared about people but somehow I couldn't reach out. Let's say that I appeared normal in every way except that there was something that kept me from being able to relate in a deep sense to anyone. During this period I was at a very low energy level. It seems that all my energy was involved in repressing all these memories. I had this feeling of being like a mechanical doll just whirling around because it couldn't get out. I remember saying to him that I wanted to reach out to people, and he said you had to experience the milk of human kindness before you can express it. This was a wonderful opportunity for me although it was very painful.

At one point, after about three years with this doctor I decided to go back to school. I figured the place for me to go was Columbia in New York. I worked during the days and went at night, and ended up staying in New York after that. This turned out to be a very hectic situation because I hadn't really finished my analysis, but the idea was that he felt that I was near enough the end that we could go on with it sometime later, but there never was any other later. I ended up staying in New York and got a job on a little magazine. That didn't last too long because there was a very repulsive overbearing man chasing me around the desk and all that usual stuff. Nowadays they have lawsuits about that sort of thing, but this was in 1946, so I quit and got a job as a secretary in a hospital. I had difficulties with my courses and dropped out of school.

My first husband was a chaplain at the hospital where I worked. That's how we met. I was his secretary. We were only married a couple of years. This was in 1948. Then we gave up and went out to Nevada and got a divorce. He didn't want a divorce, but he understood why I had to. Basically he was an only child and he was used to having his own way. He couldn't tolerate even the slightest degree of frustration. I remember things like driving through some town on a trip and we might get lost. He would go into a rage because he couldn't bear to be lost. A simple thing like that. Even though he made a good salary we always had to struggle because he spent more than he made. He could never deny himself anything. He always wanted all sorts of equipment, everything he saw in a store window or advertised he wanted it. He had to have the most, the best. The last time I saw him after we were divorced, he laughed and said, "Gee, it's a wonder I never strangled you." Because he almost had a few times. I was afraid of him, and I remember this terrible state of fear. It's not so much like he hit me, but I remember one time he pushed me down a long flight of stairs.

We had a penthouse with a terrace on West End Avenue. It got to the point where I was afraid to go out on the terrace with him, because he would just lose control. It seemed like I spent the whole time crying. What was really the handwriting on the wall for me was when I saw what was happening to me in our home movies. He would say, "I'm taking the light out of your eyes." In other words my analysis had been a total rebirth to me, I was full of joy all the time and this relationship was closing me back down. All kinds of violent things began to happen. He just couldn't stand for me to so much as dance with anybody else. He would go into a rage and start a fight. This is a very educated and intelligent man; very dynamic person, very gregarious. He knew brilliant, fascinating people. He had a psychological understanding, yet he couldn't help himself. It may be that these people he was working with only knew him in a professional way and maybe they never knew about the other side of him. It was very possible that they never knew what he was like. I saw no point in staying in that situation because I was going to be sick again. As a matter of self preservation I had to leave.

Well the man I married after, was a man I met that summer on Cape Cod. When he found out I was getting a divorce he was interested in me. He was a widower. At that time he was an executive at one of the big chemical companies in New York. He wanted to rush me into a quick marriage, but I knew I didn't want that. You find out that in a situation like this these people who think they love you madly, don't really love you at all. Their eyes are closed. They don't even see you. They plead with you, but it is an emotional dependency attachment. They think that's love, but it's not love at all.

I didn't want to marry again right away. I still had this feeling to get off somewhere.

In fact I had written my analyst to see if I could come back to see him. I could. Somehow I didn't. I had this feeling that I was going to end up marrying this other man. Actually I was in bad psychological shape after this first marriage broke up. It affected my morale. I felt very insecure, and the last thing I wanted to do was to get married right away. In the meantime this man was saying it had to be now or never. He was pressuring me. I was very vulnerable. Actually I did feel this love for him. He was a very warm, loving person and in some ways he seemed the opposite of a lot of other people I had met, but I found out later I didn't know much about him. Finally I ended up marrying him.

My second husband was very successful. Somehow I imagined that he didn't have the psychological problems. I said, "Here I found somebody who is really well and healthy, who has been able to make the most of himself and realize his potential." I soon discovered that he was completely conventional in his thinking. It seemed that his whole moral sense was based on expediency. What mattered was whether people knew certain things. Not whether things were real or true. He was extremely jealous and there were always these incidents. He used to call me up several times a day from work. He wanted an account of what I did all day; where I was all the time. Sometimes he'd be at a meeting for dinner or out and I'd invite a friend over for dinner, like a male friend, a teacher or something. Well he was terribly shocked. It never occurred to me that I was going to give up all my friends just because I was married. Or that they couldn't come.

After all we had a maid at that point who came several times a week. She served dinner and I figured, why eat alone? Some nights he had to go to business meetings. He had a lot of important things to attend. I discovered that he couldn't stand my having friends over. He was very suspicious of me. Other things. Like I wanted to have a budget so I would know how much to spend on various things. He went into a rage and said, "Well, you just want to see my bank statements!" It never occurred to me that I hadn't. I never knew how much money came in, although I had some idea. Before we were married I knew he made $80,000 a year. Later on he became one of the vice-presidents. He made more after that, but he would argue over the price of a broom. He was the kind of person that would go out to dinner and spend any amount on entertaining. He didn't want any money to be spent unless it was a form of display to impress people. That's how I finally saw it. Taking people to dinner was a show. It was always mixed with his business. If I wore a cloth coat he insisted that I wear the fur he gave me. It was all for display. It wasn't for me. It was for him.

The beginning of the end was a very strange experience. Well, I didn't know it was the beginning of the end then. Only in retrospect. After I was married to my second husband for a couple of months, we were invited to a Sunday gathering by another couple from my husband's company. We had drinks and then went over to the country club for dinner. I might have had one drink, I don't know. We were standing around in the foyer waiting to go into the dining room and a strange thing happened to me. I was talking to one of the

men, not about anything special, and all of a sudden this person's face, the eyes, a whole section of his face, . . . all of a sudden I looked up and I couldn't see his face anymore. There was this brilliant incandescent light. You know how a star looks at a distance—kind of not like an ordinary light. It was like the person's eyes were not there anymore. I was just looking at this light. I was stunned, naturally. I had never had an experience like this before in my whole life.

Something began happening to me after that experience. Gradually certain illusions about the situation, about myself were being stripped away. I suddenly knew things that I hadn't known before. I became aware of a certain clairvoyance. I was forced to know things about myself. It was a gradual sort of thing. Apparently it had its onset by this experience.

Later on other things happened. I didn't understand what this was at all. I believed that it had some kind of religious significance. I found it hard to grasp because I hadn't really been interested in religion in quite a long time, but I did feel that something was going on of a spiritual nature. I started reading Emerson and I started investigating Buddhist literature; trying to find out what was happening. But this was something that I never read about in any literature.

Other things began to happen. I was going through a period of trying to experience meditation. I had this relationship with nature that I hadn't found from the church and books or people or any of that. Sometimes I would be out in the woods or outdoors in a field and somebody would come

STREETS

GRANT BUILDING

1095

along or just appear. It would be like this person would have lost their ordinary worldly appearance. Suddenly they would be in a totally different state of being; in a radiant childlike innocence, with a different voice. When they moved they would move in a different way. Everything about them would be different. It would be like they opened up to a different center of themselves. The thing is that I wouldn't be aware of any feeling because I would be totally out of myself. Afterwards I couldn't remember anything about myself. It would happen when I was out of a self-conscious state. You realize I'm talking about something I, in this state, did not experience. It is a fraud in a way for me to tell you that this is my experience. It is not really an experience of me in my present state because I am cut off from it now. I was in a different place in every way. At the time it caused me a lot of suffering. It was really terrible, because I could never maintain seeing a person in this state of unearthly beauty. It would always change.

Part of the thing that was happening was that my relationship with my husband and the people in the company became appalling. You see, these big chemical companies, they're really out to make money. They're not necessarily honest about the findings of their chemists, the side effects of chemicals or any of those things. When I met a lot of these people, I was sort of appalled. You'd look in their eyes and you'd see this darkness. I mean that was what I was aware of then. Now it probably doesn't make any sense to you when I say it, but that's what I seemed to see in those people then. I said, "Here are all these successful people; I idealized them. I

thought, "How marvelous. No hang-ups. They've reached the top of their niche and that's what they are interested in." Later I saw it differently.

Another thing about my second husband was that my experience previous to that had been to get to know people, but with him, you couldn't question anything. He would become very upset. He was not used to dealing with his feelings. You could take off the lid and it was like there was nothing under it but chaos. It turned out that his idea of dealing with me was like the iron hand and the velvet glove—that image. He became quite successful being the way he was in his field.

I became aware that I shouldn't have married him. Gradually I lost the feeling that this was a good situation to be in. This is an example that will tell you as much about me as him. I had this beautiful old amethyst ring that my mother had given me. The stone fell out in the house and I asked my husband to call a plumber because I figured it had fallen down the drain. But he wouldn't. He refused. We argued about it. Afterwards, I mean I didn't think of it at the time. See, why didn't I get on the phone and call a plumber? Somehow or other it always seemed that these people were in charge of everything, and I never was. So maybe I never had the chance to practice that. My father and both husbands made all the decisions. Now for all the years I've been alone, I've made all my own decisions.

This second marriage didn't last very long. I wanted to have children, but I never had any from any of my marriages. There were all sorts of problems. My first husband couldn't and then it later developed that I couldn't.

STREETS

What happened with Harold was that I became totally incapable of relating to him sexually. I just couldn't. It was impossible. But I made one big mistake. I had heard they had a company psychiatrist who everyone said was a nice guy. Since he knew the family and all, I went and talked to him. Well of course a sophisticated person would know that the whole point of a company psychiatrist is to take care of the good of the company. The idea is you can be sacrificed. You are to do whatever is best for your husband or the company. He told me to go back and try to be a good wife. So I went back and tried once more but I ended up crying all night. I couldn't go against my real feelings. My husband began drinking more heavily and pounding on the door of my bedroom, then jumping in the car and racing off at three o'clock in the morning, drunk. It got to be really bad. He was falling apart drinking.

So we had this trial separation and actually we never lived together again. I was in a terrible conflict because it didn't seem right to take this man's money, but on the other hand I didn't have any money or a job. Things dragged on. Eventually he went to Reno and got the divorce himself. I let him divorce me. At the time I was conflicted about taking alimony. I didn't want any part of it. But this lawyer that was working with me put it to me this way, "Well, you can always give it back to him if you decide it is not right." I was still hesitant about what was the right thing to do. But the lawyers really pressured me into signing. They got a big piece of the action. So they did and I did. I got a lump sum plus so much a month. It didn't cost my husband anything because

STREETS

it all balances out. See I pay the taxes on it and it all comes off his taxes. But I still had this feeling that I shouldn't have taken his money. So I made an appointment and met him in a restaurant. I handed him an envelope with all the money in two bank drafts. I said, "You don't have to send me anymore." I came to the conclusion I was capable. I was trying to get my own answers. I felt this is the way I've been left and I should let it go. This is what I had to do and I did it.

After I was divorced from my second husband during the 50's I became a woman's companion to support myself. I was single nine years after that. I wasn't getting any alimony during those years. My husband died fairly soon after. His second wife never even told me until after the funeral. I guess she didn't want me to come. So I was alone and I did companion work. Sometimes I worked with children, sometimes I worked as a proofreader.

In the meantime my father was dying down in our place in West Virginia. He was dying of cancer. When I learned about his illness I decided to move closer because he needed someone to help him, but I still wanted to work and be independent. We didn't get along that well. My father had six wives in his lifetime, but he ended up with no wives, old and alone. A resident housekeeper was taking care of him.

There is another aspect of my life that I haven't gone into. Back in the 50's I had stock in the family corporation and it represented quite a bit of money. Somehow my brothers and my father had done a lot of finagling with lawyers to enable him to marry all these women and to arrange the

STREETS

alimony. My father never had to pay a penny of alimony his whole life. The idea is that they had manipulated this corporation and incorporated it so that it looked like it was the same stock and it really wasn't. They had taken a lot of the assets out, my brothers and father, but by the time I knew about it it was too late. Most of the part that was supposed to be mine was gone. I had to get lawyers to sue my own brothers and father.

I met my third husband in Washington. He worked for the Pentagon as a civilian employee. We were married about seven years. So that takes care of the 60's. I was married to him until about '67. I let him do all the final proceedings. The way it worked out was that it just sort of happened. There were so many different things going on; difficulties with his children. There was irrevocable antagonism between me and his children. They were teenagers. Their mother had died and after that they had a few years of being in charge of the house. Then I came in on their territory and of course they didn't like it. He drank heavily. And then we had to deal with his senile mother. He was supporting her partially and she was getting social security. His sister had the mother living with her and she was using most of the money. She always wanted more money. There were difficulties. Anyway she dropped the mother on our doorstep. We came home from someplace and found the mother sitting there. She was in a state! We eventually found a home for her.

The marriage fell apart when my husband got involved with this woman who was actually a friend of my aunt's. Evidently he started seeing her. I didn't know it. But one

STREETS

thing led to another, and at one point he had talked to a lawyer. He was planning to split everything fifty-fifty. But then the time came when she persuaded him to let her lawyer take the case, and he was one of these crooked types. What happened was their lawyer bought off my lawyer. I wasn't even allowed to go to the house and take my things. I didn't get alimony, I didn't get anything. I didn't get any of the furniture or any of my possessions. Before that my husband offered to bring me a U-Haul and get my things, but he wanted me to sign something for a couple thousand dollars and I was so insulted by that I just refused. That's ridiculous! I would have nothing then.

After that there were no more marriages. I had been cured. I could never marry again.

After this last divorce I went back to work as a woman's companion. At first I had a hard time getting any jobs. My skills were rusty. I worked for some periods and then I wouldn't, so gradually the money I had dwindled away. I finally went broke. I was selling the things I owned. At that point, only two or three years ago, I had a lot of different jobs, but I was on the road. I didn't have anyplace to live. This is one thing that made it difficult. I was living in the car for a couple of years. I would take live-in jobs, and I don't know, just one thing or another. It happened that a lot of those live-in jobs just end. You get into these situations and you don't know what you are getting into. One job, I took care of this elderly lady. She was 91. We lived in her little house. I did everything. I was able to save some money then. She was in good health until the end. The problem here was with the relatives. I

had found out that they had gotten her to make a new will cutting out her own sister. They were fighting over this. One day they came over, gathered up her things and took her to a nursing home. So then I was without a job. I just drove off into the sunset. Even though they fought it, I did get some unemployment compensation from that job.

Here's the point. Living in the car is not the way it sounds. The point is you drive off in your car and you have no place to stay. So you are sleeping mainly on the turnpike, at some rest stop. I didn't sleep in motels. This was the last several years. But in the meantime, it takes an awful lot of money to be on the road. Gas prices were going up, and then driving an old car that eats up oil. I was spending so much money on the car that even though I was getting $100 a week from unemployment I was using it all up. I wasn't saving any of it.

My car finally died in Connecticut. Soon after, I went broke. That's when I used up all the money I had saved from my jobs and my unemployment ran out. I found different jobs but I can't tell you; for instance, I applied for a job as a governess, but the woman fired me in one day. A lot of things went wrong. I have found that employers are just as dishonest as other people.

Well I was sort of forced to apply for welfare. That was an odd experience because you can't get welfare unless you have a place to live. I didn't have a place to live and they didn't have any place to offer. They had a place for men, a rooming house, but nothing for women. I said, "Gee, is there anyplace, a local minister that might know of anything?" So they sent me over to the Congregational

Church in Westport. They had a policy of letting people in need spend a couple of nights in their rooms on lounges or couches. It was winter and that was one of their charities. But what I needed was an address.

I kept trying to get a job. I went to the State Employment office and they evidently needed some people to fill out some CETA forms. This guy started telling me about CETA training. They needed someone in electronic assembly. I was sent to take an aptitude test. I am not very good with my hands, but unfortunately I passed. They timed you and you had to put all these things together. So I took the training and we got paid while we were training. That went on for two or three months and they let me stay at the church.

Unfortunately I never should have gotten into that training because I discovered that they had another CETA course where I could have picked up bookkeeping and practiced my typing again. But I didn't know about it and they wouldn't let me switch. They wanted to fill out this guy's class in electronic assembly. Actually I was rather awkward with my hands and I wanted to drop out, but I got excellent on all the tests. I could learn the training, but as far as doing it I had a very hard time. We did soldering and I had trouble with the fumes. When I went to visit the places where we would actually work, I found out you couldn't breathe in those places. We had been taught all these safety precautions, how to use goggles, etc. We had been shown a film about a person who went blind because the soldering particles had gotten in his eyes. Well, half of these places didn't even furnish them. The air was the worst part for me. It was like a nightmare.

GOING INSIDE

I kept saying all the time, "Don't you think I should drop out?" because I felt like a fish out of water. But they would say, "Oh, you're doing fine." See they had to have a showing of so many people in the class. Later, when I talked to the woman who had gotten me into the training in the first place, she berated me soundly for not quitting earlier; going all the way through and not getting a job. Even though I had been trying to get out the whole time. She treated me as though I was beneath contempt, because I had taken the place somebody else could have had.

I never expected to get on welfare but I ended up having to. They kept me waiting quite awhile. I had three different banking accounts with about a dollar or two in each. I had to show proof that each of these accounts was closed. That took quite awhile and I was doing a lot of traveling. I went in on a Friday with all my papers and she said "Well, it is too late now. Come back next Tuesday." I was really feeling weak, because I was hungry and I wasn't sleeping. I could hardly move one foot in front of the other and I had gone and collected all these necessary papers. I was really scared because there are times when you are facing death. I wasn't afraid of hunger, because I was used to fasting, but it was a question of all the other things adding up. This matter of being forced to move on all the time. Never getting any sleep. Being on my feet continuously. My legs started swelling up. I was having an awful time. It was a matter of trying to get some rest.

So when I told her that, she said, "Oh well, sit down and I'll see if I can do something." They do everything very reluctantly. You get the feeling that they throw as many roadblocks as they can on everything. She sent me over to the housing man and he went through a list of places and made some calls. I ended up in a hotel uptown. They were supposed to take $76 of my check but they took $79 and gave me the balance. They were supposed to give me a restaurant allowance which later, when I told them I was moving, they took away. So instead of $156 I got $123 every two weeks. It was to be filled in with food stamps, but from month to month I didn't get any. I finally got $10's worth, but then I had to ask and ask and ask. You can't imagine how many times I had to go down there and deal with the subject and stand on lines hours and hours and be insulted. They can be so rude to you.

When I moved I went down and gave them all the information. What is funny is that they were extremely efficient when it came to reducing the amount of the check, but it took weeks and weeks for them to figure out the change of address.

I stopped staying at the hotel because it was so filthy. I stayed with an old lady for awhile but that didn't work out. I'm not staying anywhere now. I sleep in some boxes with a group of other people, but my check is still mailed to the old lady's house. I don't know what is going to happen now. I have no crystal ball.

HANNA SCHAEFER

At first I lived with my mother. She was having a great many personal problems at the time and couldn't cope with anything, so when I was in sixth grade she sent me to Bay Shore to live with her sister. That was a nice home life for me and I stayed there for two years. I don't really know what my mother's problems were. She couldn't straighten out her life, her bills, her boyfriend.

When I came back she had gotten rid of her boyfriend but something had happened to me. I didn't want to go to school because I was getting pimples. I became silent and quiet and wouldn't take a bath or anything. My mother didn't understand. It got to the point where I practically couldn't do anything and my mother didn't make me. When I went to school I kept dropping to the bottom. I had no interest. I was a very confused person. My mother later signed me out to go to work.

I lived at the Simmons House (a residence for women) for a few years and during that time I had several office jobs, but I was never really happy. I started becoming depressed and started having a lot of problems. It was at that time that I met the man I have been living with for the last three years. He used to hang around the Simmons House looking for girls. When I met him I had just left my last boyfriend and I was lonely. He insisted that I move in with him right away. I didn't want to but I gave in. I was very weak then. I had no mind of my own and would allow myself to be led anywhere without really knowing what I wanted.

Things were okay for awhile but then I got pregnant and that messed everything up. I had to give up my job and I began staying home. My boyfriend really wanted to have me be like a maid in the

GOING INSIDE

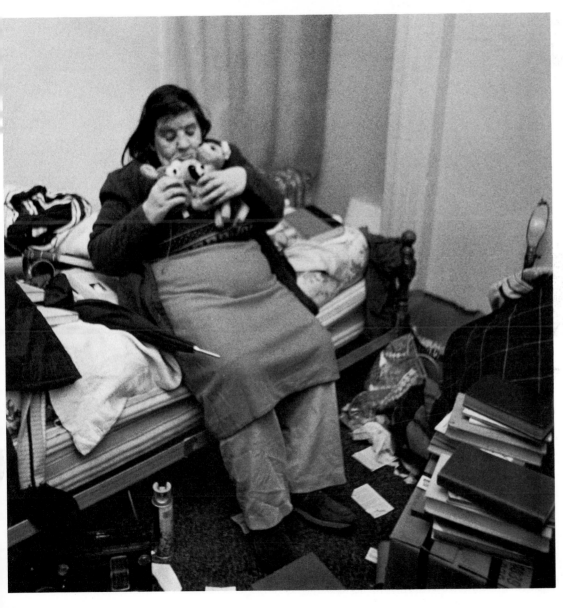

house and to have other women outside. Sometimes he would stay away the whole weekend and not say anything about where he had been. At night I never knew if he would be coming home or not. When I asked him what he did he said that it was none of my business. Getting women seemed to be all he thought about. I once heard him telling his friends that his biggest dream was to get an answering service and to come home and turn on his machine and then go out with whoever he wanted.

I felt like I was going crazy because I had no outlet. My only girlfriend was in the building and she told me that my boyfriend was trying to turn everybody against me. He was telling her that I never did anything, even the laundry, and that I was lazy and good for nothing. When I found that out, I was so hurt about the way he spoke about me that I didn't know what to do.

Everything got to be too much. That's when I tore up the furniture. One morning I just took a knife and tore it all to pieces. I couldn't take it anymore. I tried to get out but there was no choice. I had stood it for as long as I could and that morning I ripped everything to shreds. My mind was very calm, I don't even remember where my little boy was at the time. Sometimes I wonder what he saw. I know he knew something was up because later I saw him looking at the couch, just staring, like he knew something was wrong.

The police said I should see a social worker but I didn't know where to go. After that my boyfriend was saying that he was going to beat me up. I heard about a free community legal service over near where I lived so I went over there. They told me I

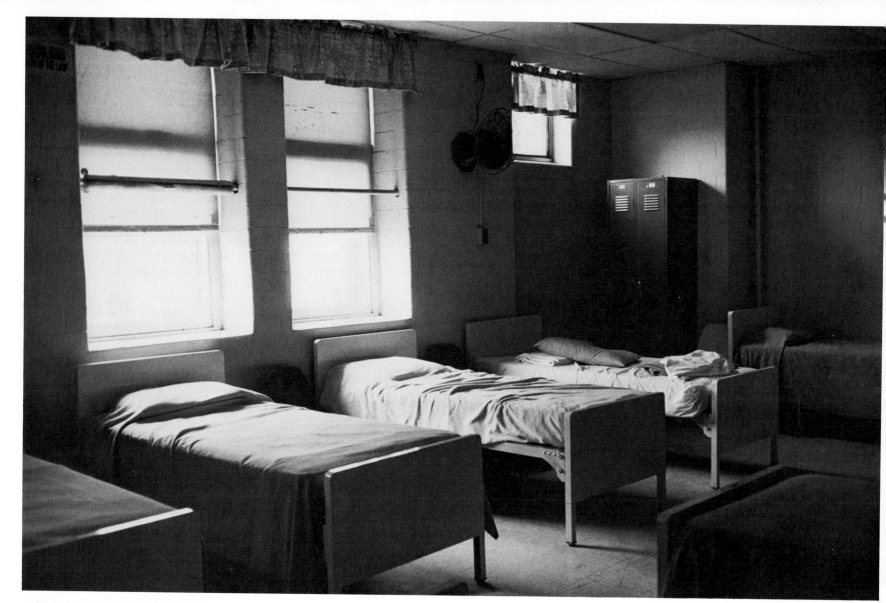

A SHELTER FOR WOMEN

should go to family court. It was difficult. I was very mixed up and I didn't know what to do. I did a lot of things wrong. I took out a paternity suit and they took away my birth certificates. I was trying to get myself on welfare at the same time, going from place to place, carrying the children. I couldn't get welfare because they said I was being supported by my boyfriend and then I didn't have my birth certificates because they were at the court and I was running all over waiting in this place and that one with the babies in my arms.

The social worker said I should come to the Women's Shelter and put the boys in foster care until I got more straightened out. So I thought that would be the best thing to do. It was pretty hard to give them up but I placed them to get self-sufficient.

The first time I got to see my boys after they were placed in foster care, I was like in another world. When I saw them I suddenly couldn't even hear what the people around me were saying, I was just staring at them. Then I had to go into the bathroom to hide my crying.

My oldest boy acted shy at first, like he didn't recognize me, but then I played with him a little and he was better. They said that the first few nights he didn't eat or sleep at all. They had a lot of trouble with him because he was so upset. The little baby, he seemed to be okay. He didn't really recognize me, but sometimes I used to make a funny little noise at him with my throat and he always made the noise back. This time when I made the noise he looked at me then he made the noise back so I guess he did recognize that.

I won't get them again until I have something to stand on, a job. The children's agency is helping me. Maybe I could get into a nurse's aide program or something as long as I don't have to go back to him. I never want to get married or live with another man again. I don't think men are necessary to me. I just want my children back and to have a home and a dog and to go to church on Sunday. The whole bit. I hope I'll get everything straightened out. I'm tired of suffering and going around in circles.

MARY LOU PRENTISS

After high school, just short of being nineteen, I went with ABC. I was in music clearance dealing with music copywriting. I had four people working under me. I got to meet wonderful people. Frank Sinatra and Sammy Davis. I got to see the Kennedy and Nixon debates. I didn't meet them but I saw them. They did one of the debates from NBC in New York. They built a set within the main studio that ran a full block. They built two small suites, just for the few hours they were there. A living room, a bathroom and a bedroom for each were installed in the studio with wall to wall carpeting. They measured both to the inch so they were exactly the same size. The minute the debate was over, it cost thousands to install, it was all dismantled.

I loved my job but the pressures were tremendous. I left thirteen years ago in '67. I wasn't fired and I didn't say in so many words that I was quitting. I just said I was so depressed. I can't pinpoint it. But if I could I could cure myself. I think my mother dying and me being alone and the pressures of the job did it. I was thirty-eight then and my mother and I lived together up until that point. I was never married, then I was alone. I was like an old clock. I just sort of ran down.

So since then, when I could find work, I worked as a housekeeper. Everyone says, "She went from ABC to housekeeping?" but it solved its problems. It's a job and a place to live when I can get it.

I don't really enjoy housekeeping, but it doesn't bother me. The last job I had was with a lady doctor and her beloved dog who I loved so. I was very happy there but I left because the dog died and I blamed her for it. He was attacked by a pack of wild dogs which sounds terrible but it's true. He was out without a leash. I don't want to talk about it.

That was out on Long Island and I just never forgave her for it. That was a year and a half ago and I haven't worked since.

I threatened suicide just after I left ABC. I took an overdose of drugs. I understand that ten pills could have done it but I took thirty. I called everybody beforehand, not to ask for help but to tell them all that I was feeling much better. I was making lunch dates for the following week. I called everybody that I could think of that might call me. But there was one friend that I missed and when she called and didn't get an answer she made them open the door. So I was taken to Roosevelt Emergency and then to intensive care. I was unconscious for four days. When a psychiatrist came to see me, he asked me if I would be willing to go to Central Islip Hospital. Of course I was so upset at being alive I said I didn't give a damn

A SHELTER FOR WOMEN

where I went, so I went out there voluntarily because I didn't give a damn. Nothing mattered. I was furious to still be alive. I still am. It's a terrible thing to say to yourself. I have no home. No place that is mine where I can go and close the door.

I arrived that first time at Central Islip on my fortieth birthday. Quite ironic, they say life begins at forty. Since then I've had a great many admissions out there. I work for a year then I get this terrible depression and I have to go back. I just stop functioning. I just sit. I know I should take a shower, wash my hands, eat. But I don't do any of this. I just reach the point where I can pack my bags and I go. I reach my desperation and I need help.

After I went in the hospital I lost my apartment. My friend put the things I wanted into storage but I couldn't keep paying the rent so I had to tell them to get rid of everything. Clothes, my books which hurt more than anything, all my mother's beautiful silver and dishes. They even charged me twenty dollars to get rid of them. I've never put down roots again.

Now I get straight disability. Not SSI. The disability is so terribly vital. This last experience, with the check being lost and the wallet stolen, has set me back terrifically. I had been shopping and made different stops. When I got home the usual thing was to put the bundles down and then see how much money was left. But there was just no wallet. Then at the same time my August check just didn't arrive. I had a room in this lady's apartment and she was always screaming poverty. So since I couldn't pay the rent, she asked me to go. My belongings had dwindled down to one big suitcase and one small

A SHELTER FOR WOMEN

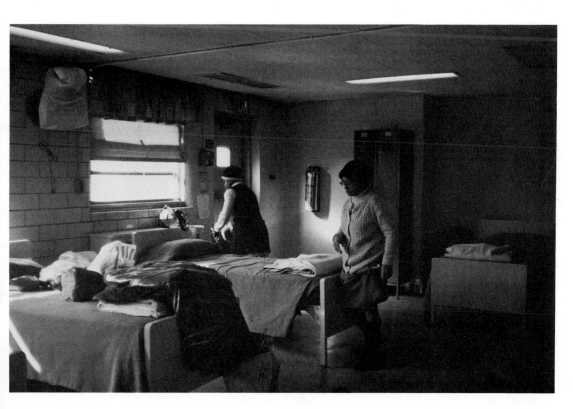

one. That's all I own. It was just a mistake
all the way around. They told me that it will
take two weeks to get it straightened out
but this is not the first time it's happened.

I don't know what I'll do now. I'm hoping
to work out something with my boyfriend
Bob. He's in an adult care home in Patch-
ogue. He's very ill with emphysema and he
has severe memory loss brought on by
drinking. Apparently it's caused by a loss of
thiamine and niacin in the system. When you
drink to great excess, the body washes them
all away and this destroys the memory, current memory. This is really nerve-wracking to
live with. He knows the past but he couldn't
possibly tell you what happened yesterday.

We met seven years ago in Central Islip.
He was a pilot for American Airlines and I
think what started his drinking was that his
eyes went. Not that he is blind by any means
but a pilot's vision has to be perfect. Bob's
heart was in flying.

I guess we don't require very much of
either one and I think he and I could be
happy together. I can cope with his memory,
maybe too well. In some ways mine is like a
steel trap, it has a lot of unpleasantness that
I wish I could forget. I guess the hardest
part would be that I just get the disability
payments. Bob has a trust and he lives on the
interest that he gets from it. But the principal
is tied up so he cannot touch it ever. It's like
a never-ending kind of thing. So the little bit
of money we need to get established in our
own home just isn't there. We lived together
for awhile in a hotel but that is such an
unsatisfactory way. We could never get an
initial start, a month's rent, a month's
security, the basic food thing for an apart-

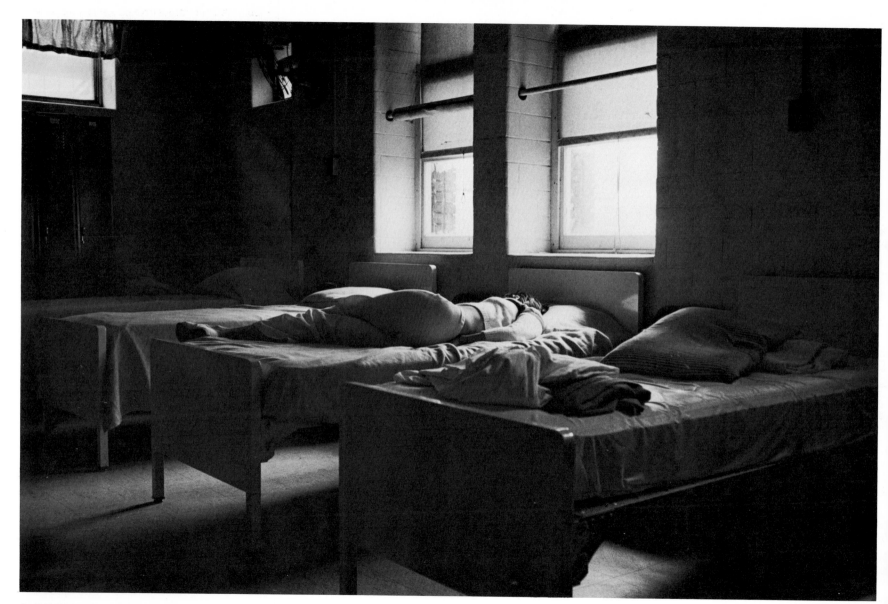

A SHELTER FOR WOMEN

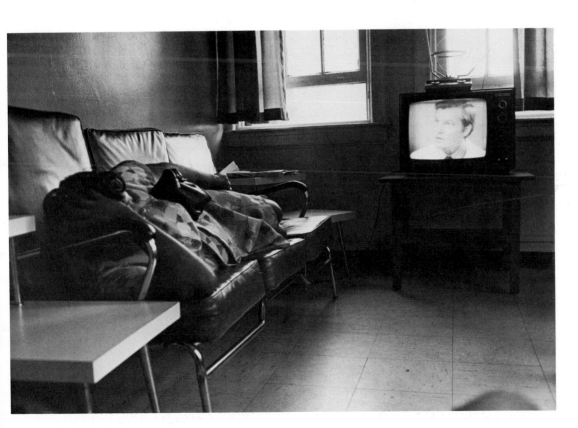

ment. It's been impossible so we've just been gypsies.

FELICIA DELLASANDRO

I went with my husband four and a half years before we were married. I was an LPN working in some of the best rest homes in Massachusetts and he was working as an usher in the South End of Boston at the Apollo Theatre. I had a room and board and one day a month off from the home. On my day off I used to press my uniforms at my mother's house, visit with her and then stop off at the theatre to see him. It was an all night theatre. Then I'd go over to his house and pick up his shirts, get them to the Chinese laundry and leave some cooking for him if I had the free time. I used to feel so sorry for him because he used to put two cans of soup together and I would say that he was going to be a sick man. He was all alone but I was keeping my eye on him.

After those four and a half years I had the funny feeling that it was time to get married. You know, I was pregnant. Three months after we were married I started to develop terrible stomach cramps. I thought I was going to die and that's when I lost my boy and girl twins that were no bigger than nothing. It took me a year to get over it. Every time I saw a baby carriage I cried my eyes out. Finally in 1954 I started carrying my son. Then in '55 I had Linda, Martha in '58, the twins in 1960 and little Felicia in 1971.

After little Felicia, my health went all down the drain. My heart started kicking out and that's when my husband got sick too.

A SHELTER FOR WOMEN

He had a stroke and his right arm became paralyzed. He couldn't talk. He regained his speech but he never regained the use of his hand. In the past five years he's gone in and out of the VA Hospital for operations, like gallstones and a leg operation. Everything's gone wrong with him.

We had separated before all that because the man wasn't much of a supporter. Every time I had a baby he'd disappear. To secure money I had to take up separation papers. I was living briefly from a little bit of money from welfare. Finally the Army made out some papers and they gave me Army money. They were giving it to the children because my husband had so many desertions that they took it away from him.

After his desertions I rented another apartment, a twin under each arm and the little ones behind me, and I paid to get the whole place fixed up. Then I got a little notice from the Army. They wanted to know if I wanted him back. They weren't giving him my address, no way, but they enclosed a note from him. The kids had seen him near the schoolyard and they were complaining that they wanted him back. I thought I'd try again.

Things were okay for awhile but then, due to ineffective wiring, the whole ceiling from the back bedroom to the bathroom fell down. Right next to my son's bedroom. It almost buried him alive. The whole place was reverberating. The skylight was coming down and the stairs were giving out. We almost didn't make it out the front door!

From there we went to a very undesirable spot the Red Cross got us at Columbia Point and that was a nightmare. The kids

A SHELTER FOR WOMEN

were getting beaten up in the schoolyard.
When I went to pay the rent they would
sneak up behind you and steal your money.
After little Felicia was born, my husband
somehow changed the money from the Army
into his name and I figured he was going to
stay with us. But shortly after that he just
departed and left us in that wild vicinity.

I put in for a transfer for close to five
years and never got it. They kept saying
that they would transfer us but we kept getting nowhere. One night we were all sitting in
the front room and we were kind of scared
about everything. One of my twins was sleeping in a chair with a blanket and suddenly
she said, "Mama! There's somebody at the
window!" I looked up and saw three black
men with long stiletto knives, dressed in dark
clothes, bending over the railing and looking
into our window. I saw that the window was
opened this much and I didn't have time to
close it. I was scared to death and I finally
started screaming, "Get away from here! Get
away!" Finally, luckily, the man upstairs
drove them away. They jumped over the rail
and were gone.

The next morning I wasn't taking any
chances. I went over to my married daughter's and she called up City Hall. Due to the
mayor we got into the D Street projects
which turned out to be even worse. We had
all kinds of trouble there. One day one of the
twins was acting up and my son slapped her.
She was only ten or eleven at the time. Her
girlfriend was standing at the door and she
ran out and called the police. The police
came and I said, "You're making a mountain
out of a mole hill. He slapped her because
she swore. It was a foul word." I said.

A SHELTER FOR WOMEN

"There's no trouble. We can handle it ourselves." But it didn't work out that way. The girls went over to their girlfriend's house and from there they went to, ah, I don't know what you call it, but they said they didn't want to come home anymore if their brother was in the apartment. They said they were afraid of him. So the police took him into juvenile custody or something like that and put the girls into foster homes. It was too bad because my son had gone to work and was paying the extra money and trying to support the house. So then all I had left was Martha and the little one.

Later Martha met her father on the street and he looked sick and all. She said, "Guess who I brought home?" He did look pretty bad so I let him stay for awhile. But it didn't work out again because he wasn't tossing in any money. He was taking from us and every time he got his check, I never saw any of the money. That was putting us in arrears. I used to say to him, "You know I pay the rent here. I pay for the food and when your check comes you should toss in a little." I tried to put that over but it didn't work. So, as I said, I had to kick him out and soon after that, due to getting behind in the rent, we were evicted.

When the twins and my son were gone and Martha had left, my married daughter said, "Why don't you send the little one down to see me?" That's when I lost little Felicia. I let her go. Then I was evicted again, because when Felicia went they cut my welfare in half, and I couldn't pay the rent. I lost all my furniture and everything. The married one said. "Why don't you come up and live with us?" So I decided to go. She was living way outside Boston and said that

A SHELTER FOR WOMEN

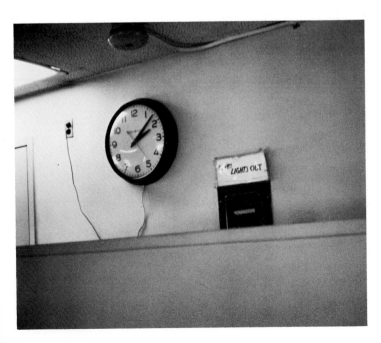

it would be no trouble at all. So I payed up the bills I owed and bought new clothes. When I was ready, I called her on the phone and she said, "We've changed our minds. We don't think it would be good for the little one." I went and got a room by myself ever since then.

When they chopped my Social Security in half, I appealed to welfare. I said I can't live on that little bit of money. I filled out all kinds of papers and they didn't give me a thing there either. So now I have to live on sixty-six dollars from Social Security and fifty-three dollars from the Veterans. Luckily I was able to find a place in Cambridge for twenty-three dollars but this month my Veterans money didn't come. They said they sent the check out but I didn't get it. I couldn't just stay in the room and starve to death and I don't know anybody to ask for money. I had nothing to eat on so I got back my last week's rent. Then I spent three nights at a shelter in Cambridge but that's all you can stay there and now I've been a week at Rosie's Place so my time is up here too. I don't have no place to stay till the first comes. Meanwhile I haven't got one red cent, so you might see me sleeping on a park bench tonight.

ELIZABETH MAIZE

I'm fifty-two now. I was born in Liverpool, England. I grew up and went to school there. My mother had seventeen children and eleven lived. My father was an alcoholic. It was like this.

In the paper there were jobs in America.

A friend of mine came over here and I got a letter saying that I should come too. So I decided to chance it. I got a job as a nurse's aide and then I worked for many years as a live-in housekeeper until I met my husband. He was sixty-five at the time but I didn't know it. You couldn't tell because he carried it well. We were married for five years when he got sick. Cancer in the throat and lung. In the hospital they were giving him very poor treatment and so I took him out and he died under my care.

After that I couldn't stay home. A lot of things happened. I was alone, then I was missing for a week. When I finally came back I sold the house but the property was gypped out of me. I had a hard time because it's not the same when you lose a husband. When you've got a husband, you've got a man at your back, but when you've got no man it's hard.

I haven't had any work in the last four years. Since the inflation, there was no work. I supported myself with the money I got from the house but then it ran out. Then I was refused welfare because I don't have all my papers. The landlady gave me notice and I got evicted from my apartment. After that I was walking the streets.

I suffer from a thyroid condition and my legs were swollen because I'd walked so much. I'd sit down sometimes but the police would tell you to move on. One police beat me. I haven't forgotten it because I was sitting on the church steps. I said, "I'm not doing anything wrong," but he put my hand up my back.

I found the Women's Shelter through Lenox Hill Hospital. They treated my legs. I asked the doctor to help me because I was

walking the streets and he phoned the social worker. It was awful coming to the Shelter. This is a bad area. It's not safe but I was glad to get a bath.

SEVA FORREST

I came to New York City with my mother from Taos, New Mexico when I was little many years ago. We were very close. My ancestors were Indian and we knew there was a need for the tribe to have help for our nation. So we came to see if we could get any extra help. We didn't wait for the so-called government to help us. Mother earned money from handicrafts and sent some back to the tribe.

She's gone many years but it's just as if I saw her now. She was sitting like this and she had just about this much crochet to finish when her face went terrible. She tried to get up from her rocking chair as if to hold me. I jumped up and got her. They say it was her heart. My people know one thing. We're not always going to be a young tree that won't get frost on our knees.

So then I was alone with my little kitten cat and dog. Comes the night of the blackout in the summer and robbers broke in everything and slapped me, and beat me, and kicked me, and tried to hurt me. I don't know them. I never saw them before. Why did they come?

I thought World War II was bad but this is worse. Whoever is giving them this dope and these things, they're killing us. They

murder up the city. If you murder a city, you murder a nation. In my religion we believe that creative love is the oil that lights the lamp of life. When we love, the door is open. If I'm making up a plan to hurt you, I've got to say, "Oh, will somebody please find me out?" If I do a harm and you are not doing me a harm then I do more harm to me than to you. But still it makes me grieve. It should not have been done.

When they came in the door I tried to get out. The little ones ran but since then I have not found them. I don't know, I was in the hospital for a long time. When I came out all of my things and my apartment were gone because I did not pay the rent. I could not find kitten cat and dog. I went to Mary House but there was no room. They sent me to the Women's Shelter and now they say they're going to put me in a home. That's worse than being dead. I'd rather live outside than to go into one of those places.

SELMA LYONS

You see the thing was like my mother. She had a problem drinking and she didn't get along with my Dad. So when they split up the family they just made the kids the wards of the court. There were nine of us and I was right in the middle.

My younger brothers and sisters went to the orphan home, but I got sent up. You know you're supposed to get a trial of some sort before they send you to the state hospital but I didn't get one. I never saw the judge. They just decided to send me up. They didn't say why. Fact is, they didn't say much of anything. They just said something about going for a nice long ride and enjoying the scenery. They took me up there but didn't tell me where I was until they locked me up.

After I got there the doctor that talked to me got madder than hell at them for bringing me there. I was only fourteen and the other patients there were mostly either forty or fifty. One doctor said he wanted to have the person that sent me there for one hour and call him dirty names.

Most of the patients were old people and I was the only young one. That makes a big difference. I stayed in the hospital that first time for three or four months until they asked me a lot of questions and they figured I was okay. Then they sent me to a nursing home in Quincey. See in Illinois when people get out of state hospitals sometimes they send them to nursing homes with full privileges and all.

But then my mother started coming around and asking for my money and stuff. She told me to come over to see her, so I went and brought her a sack of groceries. She didn't like me staying at the home and I just figured, well, I'll stay with her. So I stayed there and all of a sudden a policeman came down saying that he was going to take me to jail because I was still a ward of the court, see. And I wasn't supposed to be at my mother's. Of course I didn't know because the law don't tell kids anything anyway.

So they took me to jail and they had a new judge. He said, "You ain't guilty of nothing, there's no charges against you," and he said, "I got some real nice people where you can live real nice, that'll treat you right, treat you decent and everything." So he in-

troduced me to the Parsons and the Parsons decided to get me a job. He was a guy that worked for the state and he went around helping teenagers get jobs. He just loved teenagers, working day and night to help them. He got me a job at the Pepsi-Cola plant working on an assembly line sorting bottles. I stayed there about four months and then the boss said I wasn't able to keep up, you know, work fast enough. But he said, being as he liked me he'd keep me a month longer because he hated to, you know, see me go.

Later on when I was older they let me go to St. Louis to live with my mother in the boarding house she ran. I lived there for awhile but my mother had a drinking problem. I couldn't understand her too well, so one night I decided to go to Kansas. When they picked me up there and then found out I was once in a state hospital, they kept me in Kansas. After three months they transferred me back to the hospital in Illinois.

_____

At the hospital they sent me out to a workshop where I folded bags and put them in a little packet. I got eighteen dollars a month but I didn't keep my money, I did good deeds. See, I lived on a ward where nobody had soda or cigarettes, nothing. So I'd go out and bring somebody back a jar of coffee and we'd have coffee and play cards. I don't like any kind of institution but I figure if I'm going to live there I'm going to do good to the patients.

_____

One time I decided to go to San Francisco. I cashed my social security check and got a bus. It was a nice trip. I went to look at the ocean, sat on the beach for awhile and had a

cheese sandwich with several different kinds of cheese and French bread. That was real nice but when I was in the bus station I left my purse on the bench and went over to look out the window. When I came back it was gone and so I didn't have another cent left.

After awhile a policeman comes over to me real nice and he says, "Anything I can do for you?" I said, "No I don't want to tell you my problems. I don't want to cause you any trouble but back home everybody talks about California. How great California is." He said, "You'd better believe that California's great! We help people and the people help us. Now, is there anything I can do for you?" And I told him that I lost my purse and he said, "Well I'll just send you over to this Catholic place. They'll keep you till your check comes or else they'll send you to another place until you can get back on your feet." So I went to the Catholic place and they kept me for awhile but then they sent me back to Illinois.

_____

It's horrible in the home. When they put you in an institution they practically destroy your life completely. When you are young and have to be around people who are old, you figure that you can be classified with them. It gets to you. Here I am, haven't done anything wrong, haven't been anywhere, except for a few times, but I have to spend all my life in institutions. Well I just won't be putting anything into life. I won't be getting anything out.

Like one time a patient in the home used to talk a lot about New York. So I thought, well, I'll go there. I always heard about a store called Macy's and they said it was a block long and I thought I'd like to see that. So the buses had a fifty dollar special. Usually it cost a hundred dollars to go to New York but they had a special where you could go anywhere for fifty. I thought I'm never going to have this bargain again probably in my life, so I might as well take it now. I cashed in my SSI check again and came to New York.

I didn't pack much. I just took what I wanted to take and left everything else there. I didn't tell anyone because every time you'd start to talk about doing something they'd talk you out of it. So I never mentioned nothing. Every time anyone gets inspired to do something or be something at the home, they talk so much that you end up not being anything or doing anything, and that's why you'd give up. So I never talked much.

My money was stolen on the bus I think. I forgot to close my purse and I left it on the chair next to me and there was a kid right across the way. Later on, about ten minutes later, I was going to smoke a cigarette and I looked in my purse and the money was gone. All I had was a dollar bill.

So when I got to New York I went up to an officer and told him that my money was stolen. He referred me to a place where people sit all night long. It was a small room with people sleeping on chairs. The next morning they sent me to welfare but welfare refused to help me because I was on SSI. I couldn't get in at first but I did after a few days.

You see, it's practically impossible for me to get out of this situation. The only other choice I have is spending the whole year with a bunch of mental patients working for seven dollars a week. That's it. That's not a job, that's nothing. They give you a little work but they don't give you no real education so you could get a job and hold onto it and keep it. There is nothing that you'd really like to do, that paid money, where you could buy all the things you needed, like personal items and then have twenty-five dollars a week to put in the bank. There isn't really nothing like that, nothing for me. Just institutions.

If I could have anything the way I want it I'd like to be a millionaire three times over and I'd like to travel in style, have the best clothes there is, not just any clothes but you know top clothes, and I'd like to socialize with great people and go to school where I'd have a better education and talk just as good as the next person. That would be so good. So I'd have a real normal happy life.

JEAN LOUISE COLLINS

When I first came to New York I went to the hospital because I had a very bad eye infection. I've always had trouble with it. I was born with a birth defect. Eye muscle deterioration disease. I have had eye specialists since the day I was born, and they had already taken out all the muscles and the optic nerve because they were totally rotted. There is nothing left in here but scar tissue. When they looked at it they told me that the eye had to come out because if it didn't the infection would spread to my good eye. My eye has been through so many changes that there was nothing they could do. Some-

times when I have all these operations and things, with so many changes happening, I feel like saying, "Here take it out! Put it on a tray. You can have it. Keep it! I don't want it anymore!"

But it's definite, they have to take it out. And that's kind of a scary thing in a way because you don't know what might happen to the other eye. They don't know for sure. They give it a 50-50 chance. See, as long as that bad eye stays in, I'm not sure what's going to happen. You might as well say that I've had a messed up life all the way around.

They told me that it would cost $700.00, and I knew that I couldn't get any money from my family. My mother's on welfare and there was no way that she could get the money together for me. So when I found out that I needed the operation I had to try and get the money myself. I got some of it but not all of it on the streets. I was a prostitute. But I got tired of that and when I met my boyfriend I ended up telling him that I did it because I had to, you know, there were definite reasons. He didn't mind it. He said it was alright and that he wouldn't ask me to do anything like that for him.

I met him and we were together for quite a long time. He's black but color makes no difference to me, Age makes no difference either because it's what's you got upstairs that counts. You could be a fifty-year-old man now and I could be twenty but you see, the ages make no difference. If you carry yourself the way you should, well that's what a woman looks for in a man. We were together a long time until he started messing up.

He was shooting dope, doing coke. I didn't know about it for a long time but then he would start to come home and he would have changes in his attitude. He would jump down my throat for nothing, just start fighting and arguing. And then he'd stop and everything would be just fine. So he'd start and stop, start and stop. Then he wanted me to go back on the streets. I don't know.

One night he went out drinking and he came home and got into a really big fight with the landlord, then he settled down. I told him that I was going out to the store and that I'd be back in a couple of minutes. He was fine, nothing wrong. No sooner did I get back from the store than he's downstairs fighting again. I told him to get back upstairs and cool down, to never mind what they were fighting about. I told him if he hit the man then he'd go to jail.

Then he told me that it was none of my business and that I should shut my mouth. But it was my business because I had to live there too. Pretty soon he comes up and starts calling me a bunch of this and that and all of a sudden, the next thing I know, I'm getting hit. I'm actually getting knocked around the house, getting beaten up. I didn't know what he was doing it for. I didn't do anything. That's when I saw these little marks on his arm. I had never noticed them because he wore long-sleeved shirts. I asked him what they were and he told me that it was something else that was none of my business. I told him that it was my business, that I was supposed to be his woman and he was my man. I told him that I wanted to know about anything he did. I said, "Listen, you can mess around with that bullshit if you want to but one of these days you're going to OD or something. Someone's going to give you something telling you

it's good and you're going to put it in your arm and you won't live to see any daylight."

But he's still hitting me, putting me down on the bed, sitting on top of me, trying to hit my face and everything. My arm got black and blue up to here but I didn't give him much of a chance to really hit me. I was screaming but nobody came at all and that made me so mad. He finally stopped and went to sleep. I told him earlier that if he didn't change his attitudes then I was going to leave. I told him that he'd better start straightening up and flying right. I was not going to put up with the changes he was putting me through. I was trying to hold down my job and everything.

After that night he got worse and worse. He threatened to kill me. He'd say, "Bitch, I'm going to kill you." And I'd answer, "Look, if you want to, go ahead but you're just going to find yourself winding up in jail." Now I can't really say that I wasn't scared. You know that I was scared. Wow! He had a knife to my neck and everything. But you can get to the point when you're so scared that you just tell them to go ahead and do it, get it over with. When I told him that he took that knife and threw it down on the floor . . . And I asked him, "Now why are you beating me up?" And he'd say, "Because you bother me."

You see before he started that he was alright. He was a very lovable person, a good person to be with. But when he started, he became a living terror, a monster. I told him that if he didn't clean himself up, I was going back to Massachusetts. I believe in the saying that if you're going to tell someone to clean up their backyard, you'd better make sure that yours is clean first. I told him

to think about his own problems first before telling me about mine because there was plenty wrong with him.

I gave him fair warning but nothing changed. Finally I waited until he fell asleep one night and then I got out of the house. I took what I had on, that was it. I had no money. I was just walking around, then I met this guy. We didn't do anything. I guess I must have looked bad in my face, really sad because he apparently knew that something was wrong. We rode out to New Jersey because he had to go there on some business. Since he was going anyways, he asked me if I wanted to ride with him. I really don't know what his business was. I just waited for him to come back to the car. This was the middle of the night and I needed some time to figure out what I was going to do. Then we came back to the city again. I wasn't afraid to get in his car because he really didn't look like the type of guy that would do anything. He wasn't an evil type of person. You see, that's the way I am. I can look at a person and tell how they are in a minute. How they're going to act and all that. People think I'm crazy like that but I'm not.

After I got back I went over to Compass House and they called the Shelter and they explained the situation and they told them to send me down. I came yesterday and I guess that's how I'm here right now. For how long, I just don't know.

Right now I'm trying to get on welfare because I've been unemployed since April. That's a long time. See, the social worker downstairs asked me how I was supporting myself and I couldn't tell her that I used to be on the streets doing one of those numbers. If I go down to welfare and tell them about

TRAIN STATION, NEW YORK

that they are going to think that I'm crazy. They tell me I don't need welfare. But I don't want to be forced back into that type of thing again. I do need welfare but they are not going to look at it like that.

So I told the worker that my guy was supporting me. Now they tell me that I need to get a letter from him. I told her she was crazy if she wanted me to do that. I'm here because I was getting beat up and now I'm supposed to get a letter from him? There's no way. That would start all the problems again, I know. He's got a very short temper and I'm not going back to him. What if I wake up one morning and there's this dead body laying next to me? What am I going to do? If I associated with him at all, they're going to think that I'm doing drugs too, even though I never got into that at all. I don't even drink much. When I go out I get a Coke. I had enough of needles and drugs when I was a kid. That's one thing that I will not do.

I did try working at the Burger King for awhile. I started in the kitchen. I'd be there hammering all that food and putting the french fries in grease. The grease would be splattering all over the floor so it would be real easy for me to slip and fall. One day the boss saw the problems with my eyes and he said that if I got injured on the job that their insurance policies wouldn't be able to cover me. So he let me go.

I went to another Burger King and worked as a cashier. They had to have somebody there who was good with money and I knew how to ring things in right. Once they said that I was eighteen dollars short and that means that you are automatically terminated. I knew it wasn't true and the next day they came in and said it was their mistake.

But they make you work slave hours there. Then you only get about thirty-five or forty dollars a week after they take out the taxes. If you want overtime or need a couple of extra hours at the end of the week just to have a little money left, they won't give it to you. I've never known anybody that worked at Burger King for more than one or two months. They do enough stuff to you so that you get fed up and want to go. If you put in fourteen hours, you only get paid for seven. You don't get paid for the other seven until your next paycheck comes out. They try to jam people down there, so I quit.

Right now I need to get settled. A lot of the centers won't accept anyone over twenty-one and anyplace other than that will ask me about this man and they'll say I did something to provoke him. Like it's always the woman's fault. What that guy did to me started turning me against men in general. I started hating them, all of them, you know what I mean. But I really can't do that because it's wrong. What one man did to me doesn't mean that every man is the same.

I know that everything I've been trying to do hasn't been done yet. The surgery definitely has to happen. The eye has to come out, there's no question there, but first I need stability. An apartment. When I go to the hospital I want to know that when I get out I'll have a place to go. I need a roof over my head that I'll know is mine.

ADELE RAIFFER

When I started reading the New Testament I certainly wasn't seeking God, and probably 95 percent of my fellow students weren't either. But I began hearing the words of Jesus and I saw that I was not cleansed in the eyes of the Lord. That was when I got really upset and found that I couldn't cope. I thought that I was mad. It was at this time that I decided to jump out of the window. I know that it was pretty dumb but it was a very definite decision. I ended up staying in the local infirmary for awhile and then they put me in a mental hospital for two years.

When they let me out I moved into a hotel and lived there for a long time, but I had a great many emotional problems and had been drinking for five years. I was pretty unhappy there. Everyone was an alcoholic like myself and the discipline wasn't great. But I still felt that I had accepted Jesus as the truth and the only salvation, so I was drawn to visit a church fellowship house that was nearby.

This was a nationally organized Christian fellowship house where people lived together in very tight communal situations where they could receive the word of God. Pretty soon I decided to move in. It was a good move. They knew that living together in a tight situation often makes people grow very fast, and I did that for awhile. I grew very fast but after two weeks I had to go into the hospital again.

When I came out, I decided to go back to this house and things went pretty well until two weeks later. I started another drinking binge by drinking all the vanilla in the house. When I did that, I ran out and ran down the street and I thought, "Well, I've replaced vanilla bottles on Sunday before. This is no sweat. This is real easy." But that was it. I couldn't stand one more moment

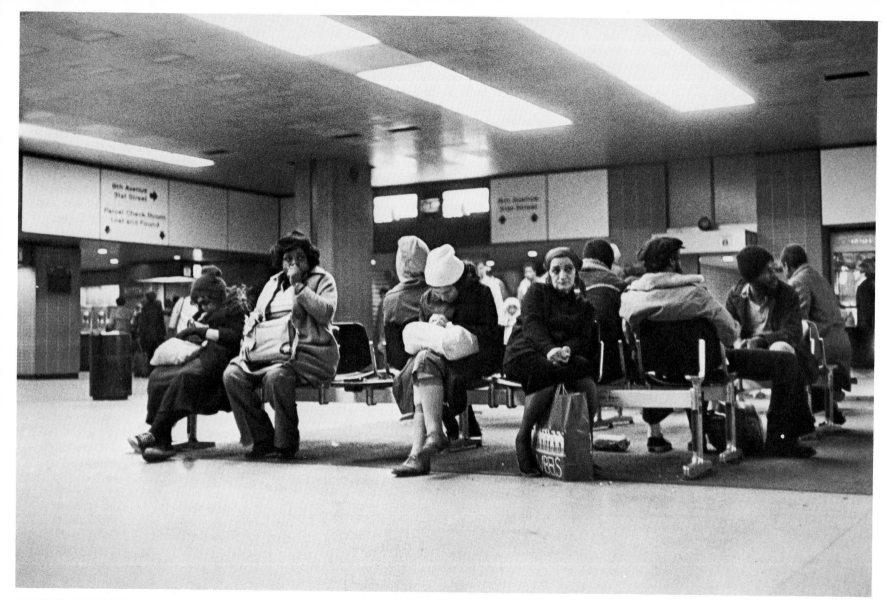

TRAIN STATION, NEW YORK

of hunting down vanilla bottles. I guess it was the love I had for the other people. So I prayed, "God, I'm too tired to drink anymore. You've just got to do something about it." And I turned around and I ran home and I told my pastor. From that day forward I didn't take a drink in that house.

After awhile I decided to leave because I had obviously been cured and no longer needed the fellowship of Christian people. I thought I could do well enough on my own and I wanted my own life. I came to New York to visit friends and I stayed with my sister and her family. I think I was pretty unhappy at the time. Pretty lost at sea. I think a lot of people come to New York to be alone with themselves, to cut off ties with the people they know. It's kind of a self-destructive thing to do, to come to New York without any concrete plans and I might have been doing that.

My sister is pretty happily married and sometimes we've been very close, but I was not finding a way to cope with people who had never met Jesus. My sister was one of those people and it became very hard for me. You see, I'm basically a back-sliding Christian. For about a year now I've kind of felt that God deserted me but his word is still pretty faithful and in my sister's house I wasn't finding a way to live. So essentially I guess I ran away. I just upped and left one day.

I stayed in the park and I wandered around for awhile. I don't remember how I found the Shelter. Maybe through the grapevine. I wasn't thinking too clearly then. I'm hoping to get on welfare or maybe I could get a job as a salesgirl somewhere.

Fortunately or unfortunately I don't

TRAIN STATION, NEW YORK

drink anymore. It doesn't seem to be a problem. There are too many other things to occupy my mind. Occasionally when I get desperate, I head for a bar but usually I stop in midstream and change my mind. I'm really not very happy about living here but there doesn't seem to be anything else I can do. I'll be okay as long as my drinking problem doesn't come back. I'm waiting for the will of the Lord.

ELLIE FREDRICKS

This is what happened: Me and my husband were going through some changes. He was going with this married woman. He was in love with her. I said if you want her, you want her, but we stayed together awhile for the children's sakes. For appearance's sake. He was messing around with her, staying out all night, coming home when he was good and ready. I'd be worried out of my mind thinking something had happened to him.

Her husband caught them together one day but he just walked out, slammed the door. Then he waited awhile and came over to my house and banged on the door. "Is Benny home?" I said, "No, he's not." "I want to see him now!" I said, "He's not here and you're not getting in here." He said, "Okay, I don't have no qualms with you." But he waited outside to see if my husband would come back. I didn't know what was going to happen. I was so nervous. I told the kids to stay away from the windows because this guy might have a gun. My husband had one too. He had a double-barreled shotgun which he didn't use for killing people. He used it

TRAIN STATION, NEW YORK

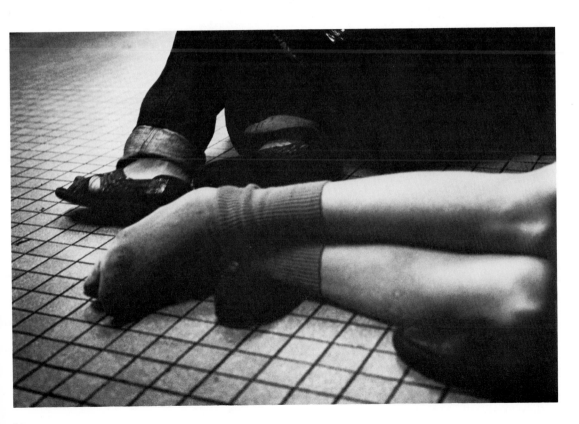

for hunting, killing pheasants, rabbits. This was in Detroit.

So the guy was waiting in the vestibule when my husband came home. I heard the man's mouth. "What do you think you're doing over there with my wife? Have you ever seen me with your old lady? Did I ever try to touch her?" My husband said no. The next thing I heard was a punch. I don't know who punched who. I was scared to open the door. I didn't know if the man had a gun and I didn't want to get hurt or the children to get hurt. They all cuddled behind me. I'm scared, I'm praying, everything. He said, "I'm not going to kill you 'cause that would be pointless. You're not even worth it. Besides it's not you I'm thinking of, it's Ellie and the children. You're their father and they need you. Not because of you, so don't think it, Benny."

I think my man was scared because I could hear a rumbling in his voice. I said to myself, "You're getting yours, God is punishing you. He knows I'm a good woman to you and I ain't done anything wrong, pulling anything over on you."

So the man left and went home. Then him and his wife got into it. Talk gets around. The same lady that helps me with my children came over and told me about it. The man beat on his wife's behind. He didn't kill her, he just beat her. Not badly. Just enough to knock some sense into her or let her know that she had to be punished. He didn't have to leave her or go out and mess with other women just because she fooled around. He just taught her a lesson and she cut it out.

You see, my husband started hitting me

TRAIN STATION, NEW YORK

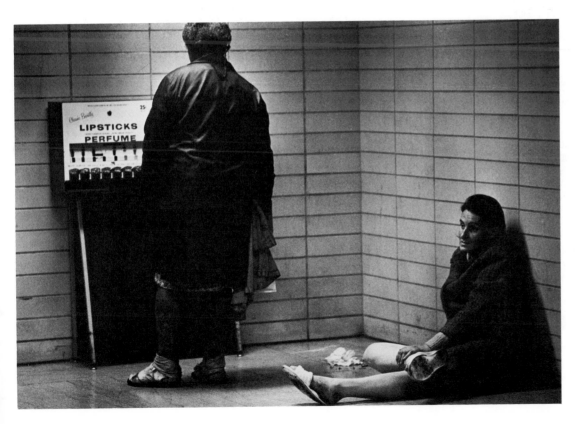

about three years after we were married. Men kept saying what a beautiful wife he had. He started getting jealous. So that's when he said, "I'm going to put her under lock and key. Then nobody can say this. She won't get her head so swelled up and take off." What I think my husband was afraid of was that somebody might wise me up. "Ellie, you don't have to stay there and get pregnant all your life and be in love with a man who's not in love with you. Cooking meals, breaking your neck, cleaning house, keeping the children. So that's why he didn't want anybody to come and see me.

But I hated it. I wasn't a violent person. He'd slap me and then I'd start crying. I had bruises all over my face. I remember one time, Benji was only about six years old and his father pulled a gun and aimed it at me. It was loaded and Benji jumped between us. He said, "Daddy, if you shoot Mama and I grow up, I'll kill you." My husband looked at me. "Are you for real? Do you know who you are talking to?" Benji says, "Yep. I love my mother and I love you too, but I don't want you to hurt her."

I got married when I was eighteen. That was in '63, so I left school. I was in the eighth grade because I stayed back a lot. I can read and write and spell. I'm not too good at arithmetic, but I can get over. I had children right away and doctors found out I was a fast breeder. They said, "Well she is Puerto Rican and maybe that has something to do with it. They have babies like hotcakes." But I love children, dogs, cats and the whole works. Before I left New York City for Detroit I went to the hospital because my mother asked them to tie my tubes. She said

TRAIN STATION, NEW YORK

I was having babies too fast. The doctor said, "No. She's too young and without her husband's consent we can do nothing." But my husband wouldn't sign the papers. He thought it was a crime.

Finally I knew he was going to kill me. One day he started messing with my neighbor, Betty, who was trying to come over and see me. She would fill me in on the happenings and that's what he would get mad about. The shows, girl talk, makeup, clothes. But he didn't want me to have no friends that could fill my mind with knowledge. He started arguing with her and he ran into the house and got the shotgun and loaded it. He says to Betty, "I'm going to blow your head off!" But her mother's right there and she says, "Now wait a minute! That's my daughter you're talking about!" Then her father steps out. He weighs about two hundred pounds and he's saying, "You said what?" So a crowd gathers and before I knew what was happening my husband was cut. Her father cut him just that fast. My husband had a shotgun and everybody knows that a bullet goes faster than a knife, but that man was better with a knife. My husband lived but he almost died. Forty-eight stitches. It was his brother who took him to the hospital. I didn't go and the police didn't come. You see, nobody called them. It was a family affair. So that night I packed up the children and went to my girlfriend's house. I told them, "We have to go now. Help Mommy be strong." I knew if I weakened I would have turned back and I don't know what would have happened because he was in a rage, on a rampage. He came back to the house that night looking for me. They said he had a gun and he was

TRAIN STATION, NEW YORK

calling my name.

The whole thing just didn't work out. Finally when we split up, the children chose to stay with him. I think they were a little confused in their minds. They were torn between him and me. They couldn't understand why we couldn't be together and why they couldn't be with both of us. But they were only children and they didn't understand this grownup business. He was a good father to them. He never beat them. I have to say that for him. He was a good father but not a good husband.

I was staying with this woman for awhile but then she had to move, and I knew that Benny had the apartment and that it was better for the children to go with him. He had a job and I was having trouble with welfare, so the boys went with him and I kept the little girl with me.

We went on like that for awhile then one day my husband phoned and said, "I'm not going to bother you. You can come and see the children and please bring the little girl." So I trust a man on his word. I went out and got the little girl all dolled up. I had her all in frills and lace and little ruffled panties. Her hair had kind of grown and I had it all braided up with little bangs in the front. I pierced her ears and gave her little rings and an ankle bracelet. Real cute because I wanted her to look something special.

I knocked on the door and said, "I'm here Benny," and I was so nervous, too! So he opens the door and he's shocked. He looks at Angelique and Angelique is the spitting image of him, big eyes like frogs' eyes, and she's looking at him and she's playing with the ribbons in her hair. I said, "Here,

TRAIN STATION, NEW YORK

take the baby." He grabs her and hugs her and I think he was beginning to cry. I think my heart went out to him. I said, "Don't cry, Benny don't cry. Let's go inside."

Her brothers were so happy to see her, their little sister. They all wanted to hold her. She was born seven pounds, eleven so you can imagine. I fed her good from the table. I made chicken broth. I wanted her to have the right nutrition with all the minerals and protein, I wanted her bones to be strong. She would get plenty of fresh milk, really good things. I took her off baby food when she was real young and I started feeding her turkey and chicken, no pork. I had her good and fat. As a matter of fact I had her so fat that the doctor told me I had to put her on a diet.

Benny and I sat down, I lit a cigarette and we started talking. He was holding the baby on one knee. She was cute looking at him but I could see she was going to cry. I could see the tears begin to trickle down her face. He said, "What's the matter with her?" I said, "Nothing. She don't remember you, that's all. Right now she's scared." so I gave her a bottle and checked to see if she was wet and changed her. He said, "You know, you're a hell of a good woman. And a real good mother too." And little Benji said, "Yes Daddy she is. You shouldn't have that other lady here." And he said, "You shut your mouth!"

It was nice to sit and talk without the fear that someone would run and get a gun, but it really didn't last long. Whenever I went away that woman would come around him or spend the night. She'd put a lot of hatred in his mind against me. Maybe he was trying to

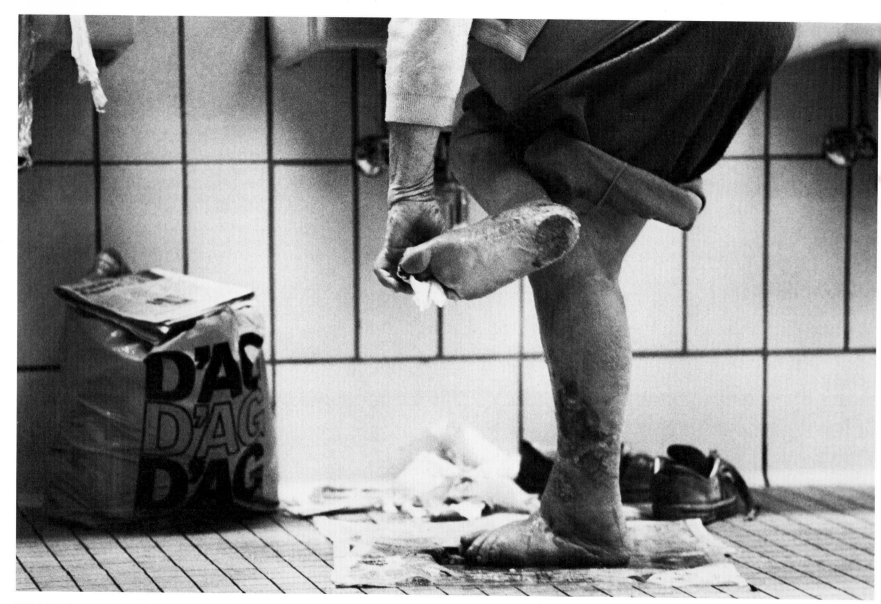

TRAIN STATION, NEW YORK

do good because he proved himself when I brought the little girl over there that day. But later he turned against me so hatefully. In a small portion of my heart I still loved the man and wanted him back, but the way things were going I didn't know how to get him back.

Finally he just got a lawyer. It seems to me that this woman had to be telling him something because I don't think he had it in his mind himself. My husband wasn't much of a thinking man. He only knew how to bulljive around. When it came to business, I was the one who handled it. Even when I was on welfare I watched the money. Nobody could say that Ellie ever spent any money on herself, or didn't buy the food for Angelique. I'd stack the cabinets full of everything. She had more than she needed plus I was saving money for her. What I'd do was put fifty cent pieces in a big old pickle jar and nobody was allowed to touch it. They respected that. Still they got a lawyer and came here one day when I was out shopping and took the baby. They convinced the lady who was baby-sitting that everything was on the up and up. So I came home and found her gone and after crying and going through all them changes I called him and asked him, "Why did you come and get Angelique? You don't know how to take care of her. That lady's not her mother. The little girl is going to grieve herself to death. She's only used to one person and that's me. She doesn't know you at all." "Well," he says, "I want her to be with her brothers."

Oh, I went to court and stuff. I didn't know how his lawyer had it rigged up, but they pulled us into private chambers and the judge asks the boys, "Who do you want to

TRAIN STATION, NEW YORK

stay with?" They said, "I want to stay with Daddy." "All of you want to stay with your Daddy?" And they all said, "Yes." I was going to cry, but maybe I was so shocked that I didn't. The judge told them to take the little girl too because there was no point in her being separated from her brothers. They all walked out of the courtroom together.

Awhile after that I met my boyfriend Gino. He was on welfare and that paid the rent and bought a little food but it didn't do much better. I told him one day that I wanted to get a job. I'm an independent woman, I don't want to be on welfare. So I went to an agency and got a factory job. The man says to me, "We've got one for you this morning. Do you want to go out?" I said, "Sure." "Okay, you catch two buses, get off at this street, walk down a couple of blocks and there you are at the factory. It's a man's factory, now remember that. No other women there, just you. Are you scared?" I said, "No, God's with me." So with a prayer I took off. My old man didn't think I could do it. He didn't think I'd like working around a bunch of men for eight hours but I did. Every time I got paid, boom, I'd bring home the money and put it on the table right in front of him. I was happy.

At the factory my job was welding. I had to stack up and weld these fifty-seven pieces together. I picked them up five at a time and I became a very strong woman. The sparks would fly but I was protected. I got a big bang out of it. I started enjoying it. I'm in a man's factory, I'm welding and I'm making some good money. The boss even came over to me one day and said, "Ellie, you're a real good worker and all the men are crazy about you but I don't mean that in a freshly way. They respect you. They like you because they say that you're a very good working woman." I said, "Yes sir, you'll never catch me over in the corner." They thought I was cute, 5'3", running around there and I was chubby too, working hard, sweating bullets.

The men had their bathroom but I didn't have one so they built me one. They fixed it up just for me with a dozen red roses. They put pink toilet paper in there, a thing of perfume and pink towels on both sides with my initials. Oh it made me so happy.

When I got home I never meant to have a bad attitude but I'd be so tired. I'd be bleeding, cut up. I'd be really worn out. Even though I'd eat I'd still be hungry, then my feet would hurt because I'd been standing all day. So when I got home I'd have to work eight hours there. I had to cook dinner, take out the garbage, walk the dog and clean the house. I had to pick up after Gino and when I got through with all that, I was in no mood for conversation. All I had time to do was take a shower and fall out. I didn't have time to make love. I was too tired.

The point is, I was out there struggling for the both of us and what hurt me most was that I wished that Gino would work and help me out. He knew how to cook. He knew his job was to walk the dog twice a day. He knew it was his job to take out the garbage but he didn't do a thing. When I got home he was stretched out on the bed. Been drinking. The house would be a mess. So I had to go into the routine again. Gino just figured that he could lean on me. Since I was in love with him I would put up with it.

He was weak minded. He wasn't strong like me and I don't think he really wanted to work. He was always used to having someone take care of him, like his father and then me. He'd just work half a day to get up enough money to buy the wine. He could never really throw himself into a job. He'd fall back on Ellie. He'd say that my sign was Taurus and that means that I'm very dependable.

So you're looking at a man who stayed home all the time and let his woman go out and work and bring home the bacon. He didn't have anything to do but bulljive around eight hours a day or sleep and drink wine. Finally I told him that if he didn't go to work I was going to leave him, but he didn't go to work and I didn't leave him. What I did do was stop working and go back on welfare. I left my job because I had to show him I was serious and that was the only way I could do it. If I had continued in the job he would have used me up, and I would have gotten sick and suffered in the end.

I guess that Gino never knew what to say or do because his mind was on welfare for so many years. That's an expression, let me explain. That means he never thought independently for himself. If a big decision was to be made, I'd do all the thinking. When I'd ask, "What do you think we should do, baby?" He'd say, "You handle it." It was the easy way out. He never had an answer for me.

Finally we split up. Right around that time I got messed up on welfare. I couldn't get the checks anymore and I couldn't get another job. So I didn't pay the rent and I got evicted. I was living in the park for about two months in June and July. Prospect Park. The police never bothered me. They would protect me. People would come and give me money for food once they got to know me. I was scared and frightened at times but nobody did nothing to me because I believed in the Lord. I'd say, every night, "God, if it's Thy will, take my life and if it's not, let me see another morning." And He did just that because I've seen a lot of mornings.

Most afternoons I'd take walks and talk to people. Truthfully speaking there was no one I could turn to for a place to stay. They all had families or no room. I'd go to the library or to a restaurant. I'd wash up in the station, wash out my clothes and then the sun would dry them. When it rained I would stay in enclosed areas. If I had the money I would probably take in a show but only if it was raining. People would give me money but never enough to get a place. Just enough to eat from day to day. Fortunately I know how to budget money, so I made it.

I tried to get into the Salvation Army before, but they only take alcoholics and old people. They didn't take a woman like me. I had to tell the truth. I couldn't go in there and say I was an alcoholic just to get a place to stay. But the Lord always answers my prayers. Like last night.

I didn't have a place to stay and I came here early, to the Shelter. But they didn't have any room, no beds left. They were filled to the brim. So they sent me down to the Emergency Assistance Unit and they said that the best they could do was to let me sleep in a chair. But I said to myself, "Oh no, I'm not going to do that," because I saw another lady there who definitely wasn't in her right mind. She had been sleeping on those chairs Lord knows how long and I said to myself, "Well I'm not her. Maybe she doesn't mind doing that because she doesn't have it all together but I've got all of mine and I'm fighting for this battle." So I asked the Lord to find me a place to stay and no sooner had I asked than the phone rings and it's the Women's Shelter calling. They just had a bed for one more. The man looked at me and I looked at him and he said, "Fortune has smiled on you." And I said, "No. God has." I got my bags and took off. See, God answers my prayers.

I want to get on welfare now so I can at least get on my feet, build a foundation. Then I can get a job. I'll be independent again, have my own apartment, pay my own bills, buy my own food, my clothes. But I don't need anyone to hurt me anymore. I need someone to love me and help me. I want a nice man to fall in love with me and I know I could fall in love with him eventually. He could work and I could work and we could build a life together.

Maybe you will go home tonight and say, "I met a girl today. Her name is Ellie Fredricks. We had a long conversation. It was very fascinating." This is what you will be thinking to yourself and good feeling will come out of it. I guess I can leave a good impression on people. I want to make people smile, make people happy.

DORIS WYKOWSKY

When I was a kid, if they asked me what I wanted to be, I always said I wanted to be a waitress. I mean, that was the most, taking account of my environment, that I could envision a woman doing. What do you do when you grow up? You become a waitress! Of course I was a waitress for awhile. I had my physical strength then. I was a fine waitress, I'm efficient and all but I'm not the smiley-smiley type. I mean, I tend to be kind of blunt and direct and I've been trying to get myself out of that habit. Do you follow me? This has been a problem on all of my jobs. If you don't smile you are going to get fired. No matter how efficient I was that was what they would tell me.

One place you had to wear a pretty pink handkerchief, all starched and everything. I didn't even have an iron let alone a pink handkerchief. But whenever I sensed I was going to be fired, I quit. They just wanted you to be flowery. After the first day there my boss wanted to go out with me and so I put two and two together. I didn't smile and I didn't have a handkerchief, so I quit.

In the '60's I had the asthma so severely that I could hardly get up the steps but I worked, getting that wheezing and doing that grueling work. I was eligible for assistance but I would not apply. I went to see a doctor and for ten dollars a week he would give me injections, vitamin injections that would help me. But that was ten dollars a week that I really couldn't afford. So I thought I would try to get enough welfare to cover the ten dollars for the doctor. I went to welfare and they told me that I had to stop working to get it.

I had a little apartment over on Avenue D. It was forty-five dollars a month and I had a refrigerator and I think I had a telephone then. They told me to get rid of the refrigerator and the phone. I said that I was ill and that the telephone might save my life some time. All I wanted was the ten dollars so I could continue working. Well, it was so screwy that I walked out.

Now that they have this Medicaid and stuff, well, they can just shove it. I still need these asthma pills but there are people finding things wrong with them just to get the aid. Doctors are ripping off the government, charging twice as much as they would normally charge. All I wanted was ten dollars to pay my doctor for the injections and the pills. Instead, I've landed up in at least a dozen hospital emergency rooms because of the asthma.

I was working until I got into a car accident. I was in Texas at the time. That's how I got on welfare. It was a pretty bad accident. Eighty little stitches across my face. Just missed the eye. It took seven years to completely heal. When I first came out I looked like Frankenstein and everyone laughed at me. I never realized until then how people are to others who are either disfigured or something. But I know my legs haven't been the same ever since either.

One day this social worker came in and told me that she would put in an application for ATD. I didn't even know what ATD was. ATD means Aid for the Totally Disabled. Then I began to realize how totally disabled I was, the stigma of it. I believed that I had to work for myself but that new label did work on my mind. What if you're a proud person? What if that proud person just has to resort to welfare?

I found out about the Women's Shelter through asking the Bowery bums. I was actually looking for a hotel room because I had just come from California and unfortunately I had been back to drinking a little. I only had the shirt on my back and ten dollars left and I could only find cheap dumpy hotels for men. One hotel was just for transients, and I thought, well I'm a transient. But the woman said that a transient was someone who was in and out. I was so innocent. I asked, "You mean in one minute and out the other minute?" It was supposed to be a joke and there's this woman there collecting money from the register and she says, "Yeah, honey, like me, I'm in then I'm out."

At that point I had no idea what I was going to do. I was exhausted. I hadn't slept all night or eaten anything and I was afraid of drinking. The bums were the only ones who would offer me information. They suggested the Salvation Army where I could at least get a meal but they would only put up men. By that time I was really mad because I'm sick and tired of that. Even in California, there's so much more available for the men who are down and out than for the women. That's because they figure a woman can always get a man. I couldn't even get a room. The cheapest hotel was twelve dollars and if that's the cheapest in the Bowery, where else are you going to look?

Through pure determination I went to the Salvation Army and asked where there was a place for women. I didn't know that there was any place like this because even in California they don't exist. So they sent me here to the Women's Shelter.

When I first came here the worker accused me of being drunk. I was agitated that day, for sure, and frightened. But when I'm drinking I'm just as rational as anyone else. So she says, "You're drunk." And I say, "What makes you think I'm drunk?" And she says, "I can smell it." Well, I could have smelled her nurse's breath too.

She finally let me stay and she gave me a dollar to go get something to eat. She told me that if I didn't smell like alcohol when I got back then I could come in. So I ate, met an interesting person, had a good conversation and then I came back. I guess the psychology of that was that if I couldn't really control my drinking I would have spent the money on alcohol.

Of course if this was a detox, I'd have to swear on a Bible that I would never take a drink. I can't tell you how many people that I have heard say, "I'm NEVER goin' ta drink again, I'm NEVER . . ." And they talk to all these social workers who don't know their ass from their elbow. They're intelligent but you just know that they don't give a goddamn because they don't know how to listen. They sign you in then they forget about you. As soon as the poor person starts rattling off their problems, and that's the main thing they need when they are like that, someone to listen to them instead of talking to a wall like always, the workers change the subject back to liquor. They ask you in a soft voice, "You're not going to take any more drinks?" And the people reply, "But a guy came up and hit me over the head and my wife died. . . ." That's when the worker goes through the ceiling.

You see, most of the drunks are sincere and they really need someplace to go to get their heads straight for a few days. They

ON THE SUBWAYS

hope to get counseling but that's usually the last thing they get. Eventually they catch onto this racket. It really isn't a racket because the drunks really do need it, but they just sober you up for three or so days and then send you out again or to an AA place. In other words they keep you in governmental enclosures. The government's paying for all of this, you know. They own the halfway houses or detox centers or stuff like that. But you could be sitting there with fifty million problems that are pertinent to you and they would say, "Get sober first. Then we'll take care of you." But you say, "My rent's due today. I have no money in the bank and they'll throw all of my things out." And those counsellors will just say, "Get sober first." So then they go out with nothing changed and go on a bender again. Afterwards they wise up a bit and they'll come in and say, "I won't drink again, I've had it. I want to go to an AA house. Let me go to the AA."

I don't know, I mean, I'm scared because I don't want to be in the position of looking for rotten hotels and living with a lot of crazy people and paying rent for it too. If I get into a place where there is no drinking allowed then I could handle that. I don't know what is better for me right now. The hotel scene, well I've seen a lot of them. But maybe I'll be lucky and hit one that has a lock on the door with a mirror in the room, where the shower isn't stopped up. Something as clean and safe as possible.

___

I have talked to psychiatrists but they just sit there and listen. I'm a natural talker. I know lots of people but I don't consider that I have any friends anymore. I never considered that I had many friends, actually. But my psychiatrist has always been waiting for the bus. When I meet one of them, they tell me to get whatever I have off my chest and they just sit there and listen. I can see the way that I got into this state, coming from a certain situation, a violent situation, was no real fault of my own. You can't deny that. But whatever has happened has happened. It is no longer a psychological problem for me. It's just a story.

You see, since I was a little kid I drank with my mother. I drank with her and then with my father. My sister didn't and that's why I hate her. There are times when I reach a certain point when I'm drinking that the alcohol gives me enough energy to feel as strong as I always wished I could be. So once I called my sister up. I tracked her down because I had lost contact with her. Long Distance. I remember that my mother said in her will, "Take care of your kid sister," and that responsibility has been haunting me. Although I'm not the black sheep, I was always the irresponsible one. I wasn't irresponsible, I took care of my family in my own way, but as an adult I haven't been able to take care of myself very well. My sister, on the other hand, is married and stable and middle class and has kids all on a bed of roses. I don't envy her in the least mind you. She has turned into a bit of a snob and I think she hates my guts. So I call her and she says, "What have you been doing Doris?" And I say, "Drinking." And she says, "Call me back when you are feeling better." Then she just hangs up. I call her long distance, spent three years worrying about her, and she did this. So, I mentally divorced her as my sister.

Well I never knew what the shakes were. I had been in a hotel and had been on a good bender and I had no money. Not really wanting money for food, I had only enough money to buy either a quart of milk or a thing of port. That was the first time I ever had the shakes. The shakes are like, you get up and you can't walk. It's like you're on a real bumpy subway train. You can't do anything. If you take another drink, they stop. And that's when you are truly, physiologically an alcoholic.

Now three quarters of the detox centers make you go through it cold turkey. If I had done that I wouldn't be talking to you now. Cold turkey, where you just vomit and shake, vomit and shake and they keep pouring tomato juice down you. And they feed you candy. So instead of drinking, you are eating candy, tomato juice and coffee all day, to make up for the depletion. You end up fifty pounds heavier, sluggish and I think, moronic and uninteresting.

You know, a pint of whiskey a day does nothing to me anymore. To get drunk on the cheap chemical wine I have to drink a half gallon. Your body does get screwed up, and that's how you get to be an alcoholic. You stop discriminating. The only help for that that I can see is never take a drink. That first drink is going to kill you.

BETTY WEISS

I live alone now. My husband died a few years ago from heart failure and there's no family. I'm on Social Security but I came here to the Shelter because of an emergency. I came to an emergency because I couldn't

ON THE SUBWAYS

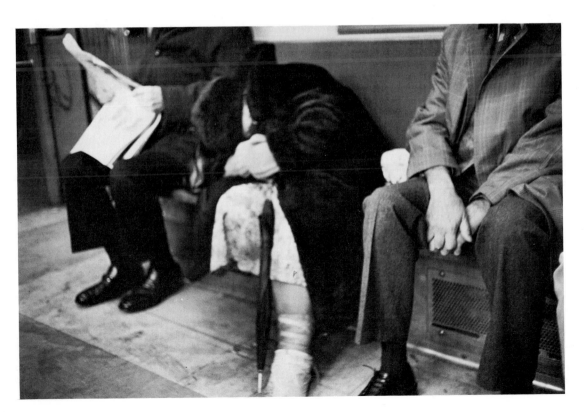

get off the trains. It was like a continuous, perpetual thing.

Usually I live in the hotels but it's too expensive. They made me pay by the day and paying by the day it was about sixty dollars a week instead of forty. My money also went for food. I didn't just spend two dollars. I spent five sometimes. You can't help it.

Well, when you run out of money you try to hold on till your next check, right? Of course I wouldn't have a place to live unless I went to a human place. If you have no money they can't give you a room for nothing. So I was living on the trains before I came here. I'd go back and forth a few times. How many times? Thirty times. I'd go to all the different lines. I'd switch from the Eighth Avenue to the BMT lines to all the different lines. Thank God they left the two toilets open in the subway stations. There were certain stations where they had toilets for women. They usually had these closed with a coinbox but thank heavens they kept one of them open.

I ate leftovers. Not too much, one or two days. And I was so mad! I couldn't imagine why, why all of this. Do you know how people act when you eat leftovers? They don't want it. No, they really want you to have money when you come into a restaurant. But I hardly ate. I hardly ate. I asked a few people to trust and it was often hard to get people to trust even for a donut and coffee. If I trust you I'll have to trust ten others, so the saying goes.

I was all over the city on the trains but then

ON THE SUBWAYS

I came to an emergency. I had the accident on my shoulder. The train wobbled something terrible and I jumped out of my seat. I never saw anything like it. A twist of my shoulder and I jumped right out of my seat and fell on my head. It was very dangerous. A kind nurse helped me to get up but I was in very bad pain. It was a displaced something. I had no idea. It was like a big bruise, a bang, a twist.

They took me to the hospital and they treated me but they didn't keep me overnight. I thought I'd have to pay. I thought, thirty-five dollars for an emergency! I didn't have any money on me at the time. I don't have anything at all! No money, and I was in very bad pain, very bad pain. They told me to go to Elmhurst Hospital. The doctor there gave me three dollars to take a cab. It was the wise thing to do, but I was hungry and I was controlled not to take the cab so I could have a little roll and butter and a cup of coffee. I remember it was at a luncheonette on the corner. So I took the trains and that lasted about eight days.

The police made me get off the trains. I was a disturbance. They said I was a disturbance. They said to go to the Emergency Assistance Unit at 250 Church Street and then I came down to the Women's Shelter. I've been here before. This is my fourth time. Twice I ran out of money and twice my checks didn't show up at all. It seems like a continuous perpetual thing. Evidently it's part of some kind of project to see what happens when you don't have any money in the City of New York. Everybody knows that if you don't have any money then you're out of luck. But this place here, the Women's Shel-

EATING

ter, this is a humanity place. This is a humanity place and the others are, you know, dollars and cents. Everybody tries to make a few on you.

ANNE JAMESON

I came to New York because I wanted to be a ballerina. I knew the greatest talent and the greatest teachers were here. All kinds of pain, agony and sadness were calling me to New York. I thought I might audition for shows but then I realized there were none for me. I just didn't know what area to go into. I had a nervous breakdown. It's a strange feeling, like you keep drawing and drawing and you have no feeling for it. You do it because you want to keep up. Then I lost my memory and I got thrown out of my apartment. I was evicted because they shut off the heat and electricity before I learned that I had to pay the bill.

I have met a lot of people who said they would help me, but they actually just wanted to take me to bed. On 42nd and 7th Avenue a man came up behind me with his hands like this and I yelled and screamed at the top of my lungs. I told him to get out of here and he took off. I know how to protect myself but I don't get violent or unfeminine unless I'm forced to. Once I met a kid in front of Penn Station who put a dollar bill on the floor. It's so obvious. Some other guy runs up and picks up the dollar bill and stands there. I told both of them to get lost. I was going to call the cops. They all figure you are out of money. The pimps wait around because they think the first thing a woman will do when she is destitute is become a hooker. Sell the body for money.

My social worker knows my case and she said she would do something to help me but it's hard to find work. The social workers really don't know about life on the streets per se. My brother-in-law is a theologian but he works as a security guard. It took him a year to find that job. So there are lots of people with PhD's out of work. Of course women are discrimninated against and I guess that made me feel like a volcano. Everything just erupted and I went absolutely mad because I never spoke up.

I was sleeping at the Welfare office. I had no money to take a train so someone told me about the Women's Shelter. At the Shelter I realized that there are a lot of people that are not really with it. They just sat and watched television. They gave me a bed next to this incredibly sick old woman who coughed all day. Then this lady had a girl in bed with her so I don't know. When they stole some books from me I had to find some place where I could do my exercises just to keep my head straight. The next thing I knew this girl started up with me: "What does she think she's doing?" They just got me so mad that I exploded and started screaming. So they sent me out. I had no place to go. Someone gave me a chart of all these Catholic organizations and they did absolutely nothing for me. They turned me away. I guess they thought I was a whore. So I came back.

I'll look for secretarial work until I get set-tled. My dream is to have my own building where I could have artists, musicians and dancers, people who are talented and want their own private spot and to be with a group. They could pay so much for a room to rehearse or whatever. Privacy, that's what I'm saying. Meanwhile I'd like to get myself a job. Get myself settled. I might possibly develop a new life style because I don't like the life style I've been living.

FRANCES BERRY

I was born on the beach of Carnarsie Shores in 1924. My mother and father lived there for several years while my father had a hack license. They had many friends that they told me about, people I was too young to know. When I grew up to the age of about three or four my mother and father encouraged me to dance in front of all these people. I would get dressed up on a Saturday night and dance and the people would throw me money.

My mother went to business school and was considered to have the most beautiful figure in Brooklyn. The men in the neighborhood described her as a Venus. She was five foot ten, slim and with beautiful legs. As I remember she had reddish brown hair and blue eyes. She looked a little like Dolores Costello. She was a real Irish beauty.

In my Catholic elementary school I was awarded a scholarship and went to McDonald High School. I stayed there two years and all my teachers wanted me to take a business course but I wanted to go into show business. The lights and all that. I regret it now. I would never have had all this diffi-

EATING

culty if I had finished high school. If I had gotten my diploma I could have taken a Civil Service test or I could have been self-employed. But as it was I only had two years of high school and you just can't get a nice white-collar job on that.

After I quit high school I became a professional dancer at Leona Neddy's. That was very, very thrilling. That was the best. I never had such a wonderful time. I never met such wonderful people. Milton Berle came in every Sunday night with his wife Joyce Matthews. Joey Adams came there and the Yankee baseball team had their steak dinners there. I knew a lot of them personally because my brother started on the same baseball team. Joe DiMaggio, the whole Yankee team would come in.

I danced in the chorus. I did a can-can dance, the Chinese number and a flipsy-daisy. Then we all had a lot of songs in the finale. The main theme of the show was "You Do Something To Me" by Irving Berlin. Every night there was a gentleman in a full dress suit who always reserved a ringside table. He said his name was Roy and he looked just like Irving Berlin. After the show he would bring me up to his apartment on Central Park. All the musicians would be there but they didn't bring their instruments. He would talk shop with them for hours. He could have been head of the union or he could have been a songwriter. I don't know.

He told me that he wanted to finance my career as a ballet dancer but I told him that I wasn't interested in ballet. The last night, when the show closed, he wasn't there. I was heartbroken. I couldn't go home to my mother because I wanted to see him. So I just walked the streets of New York.

EATING

That's when I decided to take a train to Boston. There I met a man in show business whose name was Frank. He was appearing with Olson and Johnson in Hellszapoppin. He had a mind reading act called the "Mental Marvel." He worked around a lot and we always went out to dinner together. In Boston they had the most wonderful meals, mostly specializing in fish because of the city's location near the water. They had fish dinners, fish chowder. My boyfriend used to buy me fish and chips. I got a job as a waitress in a place that had a seven course dinner special for less than two dollars. I can't remember the name of the restaurant. It wasn't far from Marlboro Street where I stayed in a theatrical hotel. I didn't continue my dancing career because I didn't get any good offers. I went around with this guy instead because he was pretty well known up there. I met Olson and Johnson and I saw Ella Logan and Carmen Miranda doing rehearsals.

I continued working as a waitress until one day I was walking along and three men lured me into a hotel, and like a fool I went. I went right into the bathroom because I was afraid that they would try to attack me or rape me. I must have blacked out. I don't remember but according to police reports I jumped out the window from one flight up and told the cops to call my father. He came up from New York to Boston and took me home.

In New York my mother put me in Bellevue Hospital mental ward. She thought that I was crazy to run away like I did. I stayed there for ten days but the only thing that was on my mind was my guy. Not the one in Boston but the one in New York, the guy I

EATING

used to see at the club. Everything that bothered me centered around him. Who he was. Where he was. I couldn't find him, I didn't even know his right name. I had been up to his place for three months and I didn't even know the address. We always went there in a taxi and I never noticed the address.

Later on I became engaged. My husband was my brother's best friend. They were both on the same baseball team with Billy Rizutto, the Yankee. My brother and I were in a flower store and my husband came in and told my brother that he would love to take me out. So my brother asked me, "Do you want to go out with my friend Christian?" And I said, "Yes." So I went to his prom. He graduated from Canson Harris with Honors. He took electrical engineering. Then he went to City College and graduated there with Honors. Then we got married because he rushed me into it. It was a nice wedding, a week before St. Valentine's Day. It was beautiful with bridesmaids, and my sister was maid of honor. We didn't go on a honeymoon because he couldn't take any time off from his job. He just took the weekend. I really didn't care about the honeymoon.

We got along pretty good. We moved into Liberty Park in Queens, a very elegant place and rented a very nice apartment. We had company all the time. He had so many friends and visitors that we'd always have a party on Saturday night. When he was in the Navy he would always bring home a bottle of Christian Brothers Port and a box of Benson's Cherries. Then I got pregnant.

One Saturday night I was getting my labor pains but I didn't want to go until he got home at eight. So he came home with the wine and cherries and I immediately said,

"Gee, I think we'd better go to the hospital." I had a black maternity dress on and a black fox fur coat. I had a valise packed with all the things I needed, things in silk and satin. I had these little sachets that my mother-in-law taught me to make. I was so dolled up. The landlord of the house said that he thought I was going to a wedding.

I can't say that taking care of a baby was what I really wanted to do. I always wanted to be some kind of star. I wanted everybody to look at me. I was that vain. I wanted to make myself the prettiest girl because I was naturally pretty. Walter Thorton wanted to use me as a model. He said I had great potential. And even though I have false teeth now most people don't know it. Anyways, we got along good. We lived in Washington D.C. and he went to Navy Intelligence School. He didn't like it because there was too much graft involved but I loved Washington and I met lots of lovely people from all over the United States. My husband kind of knew a lot of big shots and he got a lot of offers because he has brains and ability. My son was two or three then and sometimes my mother-in-law and my father-in-law would come for a visit and stay the night. I got along with them very well, I especially loved my mother-in-law.

We stayed in Washington for a year, while he was in the Navy. After that we went back to Liberty Park where my husband got a job with the Polytechnic Research and Development Company. He had a pretty good job there but he started drinking heavily. He was an alcoholic. He would come home and be very hard to live with. I couldn't please him and he became, how should I put it, a very bad influence on me.

He would tell me to get another man. He would tell me to leave. He never was the same once he began to drink but he kept his job even through all the drinking.

Even then I think he was keeping someone else. A blonde. When I was first married and my son was a little baby, my husband's father said to me, "What about the other one?" He had another woman all the time we were married. When he went to work at PRD he told me that there was this pretty blonde there who would draw pictures of him and call him a fashion plate. So maybe that was the girl he was keeping. I never saw this woman except later, when I left the house, when I decided to live alone because my husband was fighting with my son too much. My son was sixteen at the time, and they would fight because my son wouldn't report to work on time, he'd oversleep. He got his working papers and quit high school and was doing messenger work for my husband. I said that there would never be any peace in the house as long as all three of us lived there, so I made the first move.

The first thing I did was go to Chicago where I was robbed of three hundred dollars. I came back broke and my husband put me in the mental hospital. While I was there he got an annulment of our marriage. I have no idea on what grounds. To this day I have no idea. All my friends say that if he didn't serve me with papers then legally I'm still married to him. People have told me since then that you can't get an annulment after you marry and have children. You have to get a divorce.

I was there for two years and during that time he married his second wife. I didn't

DRINKING

want to be in that hospital. I knew that I wasn't off my rocker. I was just very nervous because I missed my son, I missed my house. There was even a Chinese doctor there that spoke to my husband. He must have told my husband that I wasn't mentally sick and that he wanted me to go home every weekend. So my husband came every Friday night and he took me to my brother's house. I saw his second wife once. I really don't know how long he knew her but I assume he knew her as long as he knew me.

After the two years in the hospital I went into a boarding house with an attendant. She was abusive and ignorant. A horrible human being, the worst you could ever see. Yet she had such conceit! She thought she was the most beautiful woman in the world. She would come in and put her hair in pigtails and sometimes she would walk around naked. Ugly! I had to go to the store for her. She'd give me a check and I'd have to buy her a bottle of scotch and a six-pack of beer every couple of days. She was drunk day and night.

I would have to go to the stores and get stuff for breakfast because she wouldn't make breakfast or dinner. So, many times I had breakfast out. A couple had a nice little coffee shop a few blocks up. Other times I would go to the grocer and bring home a TV dinner. I tried to forget the fact that she was mean and belligerent. She was very prejudiced too. She hated whites and yet she boarded me and this other woman. She was very cruel to us both. This other woman was extremely disturbed and had very hard luck. Her husband had left and her son was in a crazy house. When it was time to go to bed, she would be raving and talking

DRINKING

and screaming. She was completely out of this world. You couldn't talk to her when she got like that. I stayed there from early summer until after Thanksgiving.

I had a little money so I left that boarding house and I went to New York. I met a guy there in the station at six o'clock in the morning. I was putting some makeup on. He said, "You're pretty enough. You don't need any makeup. How about I take you and we get a drink? The bars aren't open but I'll get you some coffee or a soda or something." He was a handsome Irishman, so we walked from the station to the Ramada Inn for something to drink. He told me that he was a veteran and worked in the Post Office. But later he said, "I have to level with you, honey. I don't work in the Post Office. I'm Joey Gallo's right hand man. He's a gangster."

After that we used to meet quite frequently. He'd spend a hundred dollars a night. He'd drink ten Bloody Marys down just like that without batting an eyelash! We'd have something to eat and sometimes we'd go to a hotel but he was out like a light. He drank more than my husband you know. We'd go to a hotel and when I'd wake him up, he used to beg me to get him some Alka Seltzer and aspirin, getting him in shape so he could go to work. So there was very little love life between us. One night he told me that he thought it would be best if we didn't meet each other at his place anymore because he was scared. He said he was very disliked and lots of people wanted to rub Gallo's men out one by one. He was on the top of their list and he told me that if they decided to give him the shakedown I'd go right along with him. He told me if I wanted to live I'd better not see him in New

DRINKING

York anymore. I could see him in Brooklyn but not in New York. I didn't see him much after that. We made a date for New Year's but he never showed up. I never knew what happened to him.

At the Valencia where I was living on welfare in the Village, I met a nice guy by the name of Charlie. One day he asked me if I wanted to meet his best friend. I said alright, and we went over to the next hotel called the Bluejay. We went up a flight of stairs, opened the door and it looked like a rat trap. Everything was peeling and falling apart. The linoleum rug was an atrocity. It was a horrible place, unlivable. The guy sitting in the chair was Joe, but that wasn't his right name because he was wanted in another state for some felony. Anyway, he was Rocky Graziano's cousin. He looked like Rocky and both of them liked to fight. Eventually I got to be quite useful to him. I'd fix his house; I'd shop for him. I'd get him cigarettes and scotch. I didn't drink scotch but Joe would drink over a quart of scotch a day and I would mix it with milk for him. I'd have beer, soda or coffee.

Joe was the Don of the Mafia in the Village area. He was a dope pusher. He'd have runners come up every day, handsome young men. They'd come up and get the stuff and then he'd give them an address and carfare. He had a lot of money from that. He also got a Veteran's check. Actually he got a hundred dollars more because he got the Congressional Medal of Honor from President Truman for bravery. He knocked those Germans down and he killed them. He loved to kill them. You see, he was a psychopathic killer. When you parachute down behind the lines, you have to be a psychopathic killer or

DRINKING

else they won't take you. If you are soft-hearted, you can't kill. But Joe liked to kill Germans because he was from Italy. He liked to kill the Germans one by one.

One Sunday I was cleaning while he was sleeping. I was dusting and sweeping and doing the best I could and he woke up in a very bad mood. He yelled, "Look honey, you'd better do some quick thinking and if you don't answer my question, I'll throw you out the window." He was very violent and vicious and I was taking a chance just being there. He said, "Now look! You're the only one in this room. I'm missing my syringe and I'm missing my heroin. Do you have it?" I said that I didn't and offered to let him search my bag. I would never think of taking a thing like that. Later he found out that there were two lesbians who had just come out of jail and one of them who was on dope had crawled out her window, onto the fire escape, and into Joe's room. She had lifted the dope.

After that Joe wanted to take me to Chicago to meet his brothers. He told me, "Only the best go with me, baby, and you have to be investigated." I said okay. He called his lawyer up and his lawyer told him that I was a bastard, an illegitimate person with a mysterious past. He said that no one knew where I came from, from Europe or Spain or the U.S.A. Joe said that he wouldn't be caught dead with a bastard and that I could never go anywhere with him. He said, "I want you to go out that door and don't ever come back. But if you ever go to the cops or tell them anything, that will be the end of you." Well I left and was very glad to get out of there. After that I got involved with a Yugoslavian who wanted to use a butcher knife on me. I had to go to court against him but I can't tell that story, it's still too painful.

I would like to tell the story of how I fell in love in Canada. I was left a thousand dollars when my mother died so I wanted to take a trip to Canada. When I came off the train in Toronto, I saw this young gentleman. He was dark and nice looking and he said that he wanted to show me the nightlife. His name was Sonny. He told me not to worry about being alone because he was expecting his friend and his lady friend. So we go to this nightclub and his friend comes in. He was a handsome young Scotsman and he looked like Robert Stack. He had the tweed coat and the light brown curly hair and blue eyes. He came in with a nice looking brunette who had genuine leopard on her hat. Right away I was attracted to this young Scotch guy because he had a charm about him. You could tell he had a high, European education. Anyways I kept my eyes on him and his girl-friend started getting very sarcastic toward me. Sonny was getting all bothered too because I was his date and he wanted to take me home. But I wouldn't take my eyes off Larry. Sonny said, "Look, honey, you've got to let that guy alone because he's a homo." I didn't believe him but I said, "He might be a homo, but he's the man who's going to take me home because I'm in love with him."

So no matter what Sonny or this other girl said, this guy took me home. We got to my hotel and brother did we kiss! We embraced and for the first time in my life I was with a man I loved. He knew I loved him, he could feel it and he was very pas-sionate. So this went on for awhile but I thought, well he's a handsome young man, about five years younger than me, what if he woke up and I told him that I had a child. He wouldn't think much of a married woman, mother, seducing a young and eligible bachelor. So, at the height of our passion, I told him that I had to check something in the lobby and I checked out and went home. Apparently I broke his heart. I found out later that he was a songwriter. He wrote, "Cry Me A River" and "Canadian Sunset". He also wrote "It's A Sin To Tell A Lie," and there's a verse in it about me that says, "Frances is getting set to be my blushing bride."

Finally I was living with my husband's uncle on welfare. I was helping him because he isn't able to walk, but he's able to make it to the bar! When I was over there I had to wait on him. He's a very ornery old man. He's under the impression that he's a lady killer and he made several sexual advances toward me but I nipped them in the bud. He also made too many rules. It's very hard to live with an alcoholic. For example, I had to be home at dinnertime or else I couldn't get in. He'd lock the door at seven. At night he made me turn out all the lights and sit in darkness. He said he didn't want his electric bill to go up. Then he went on rampages. I once found my alarm clock broken to bits. I found the locket that my son gave me for Christmas broken to bits. He destroys all my things. That's why I left and came here to the Shelter. My social worker told me about this place when I was on welfare. Now they're looking for another place for me.

DRINKING

DRINKING

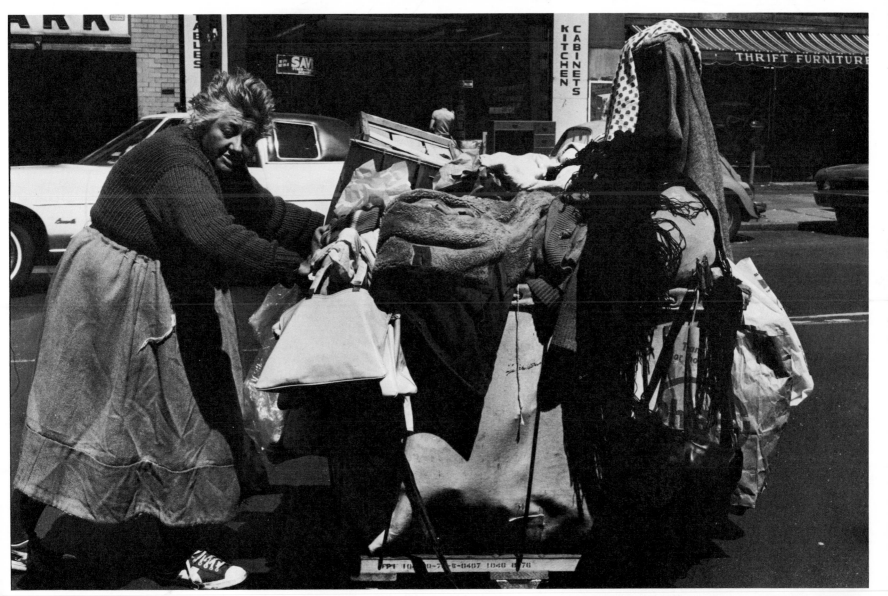

A DAY IN THE LIFE OF DARIAN MOORE

A DAY IN THE LIFE OF DARIAN MOORE

DARIAN MOORE

Darian Moore is perhaps the archetypal
shopping bag lady. She is certainly the most
photographed, and because she is extensively
interviewed by the media, she is something
of a star. Darian was released from the state
hospital to welfare care and says that she
has been living on the streets successfully for
nearly ten years. At some point, public agencies tried to settle her in an SRO hotel but
she created such a disturbance that she was
asked to leave. She has since found her own
adjustment on the streets.

On very cold days in the winter she
takes refuge in Mary House. But even there
she refuses to use a bed and sleeps on a hall-
way bench. For the most part she stays
outside and travels up and down the streets
with her huge cart.

Afternoons and evenings spent with
Darian are always interesting and eventful.
Her days are filled with the activities of
maintaining her life style. She begins her
mornings with a beauty routine: combing her
hair, applying a facial treatment, rubbing
it off, and changing her dress. During the
day she looks through each and every garbage can and rubbish pile that crosses her
path. She sits for hours at a time in her particular spots. She really enjoys company and
loves to talk to almost anyone who will pay
attention. Sometimes she will spontaneously
begin shouting at no one in particular and
will get into arguments with people who
harass her. But for the most part she is very
sweet natured, friendly and cheerful. Making
friends with Darian is easy but getting away
from her is a different matter. She always
has two more things she must finish telling

A DAY IN THE LIFE OF DARIAN MOORE

you about and just a few more errands she would like you to run. It is a fact of her life that she needs other people to help her out. Most of the food stores will not allow her inside. There is one coffee shop that will give her a glass of water and sometimes a free cup of coffee. A certain fruit stand vendor will always allow her to shop there and a Greek restaurant often gives her something to eat. But few other places will let her go inside, even if she has the money, and none will let her use the bathroom.

One evening she braved walking into a pizza parlor to get some coffee and the counter man angrily yelled at her to get out. I went back in for her and found myself in the middle of a confrontation with a furious customer. He came up to me blustering loudly, "Would you like her to come into your living room and have coffee?! Would you?!" He and the counter man fairly steamed with rage and I was taken aback to see the depth of their feeling. I said, "I only want to buy her a cup of coffee. She doesn't have anywhere else to go." After a moment everyone settled down and I talked to the man behind the counter about Darian's problems. In response he told me a long story about his own mental breakdown and recovery. The only thing that saved him, he said, was his job. I tried to explain why Darian didn't have a job and why she lived on the streets, but finally all he wanted to know was whether or not I would go out for a drink later.

In spite of her difficulties getting food, Darian eats all day long. Her diet consists almost entirely of carbohydrates. Hostess cup cakes, spaghetti and bread are her big favorites. She has very few teeth so chewing

A DAY IN THE LIFE OF DARIAN MOORE

is a problem. She gets free shish-ka-bob from a vendor, panhandles for money when she needs it, and gets one of her friends to shop for other food. Sometimes people simply hand her cigarettes and change as they walk by. She smokes incessantly and drinks enormous amounts of coffee. She likes at least four sugars (and will send you back if they are not all there).

The possessions in her postal cart consist of a whole house full of things, from pots and pans to books, shoes, magazines, toilet articles, personal papers and clothing, most of which she has made herself. Darian is a good seamstress. She uses large needles and yarn to piece together new garments for herself out of scraps of material and old clothing. She makes dresses, skirts, bloomers, quilts and even coats. She attempts to sell them to passersby. Some people stop to chat and give her money but few will take the article she is selling.

Her cart, which looks like it couldn't possibly hold another thing, constantly has new articles piled on and tied to the top or sides. She carries all the necessary items for her daily existence, including a dining table. This is a small wooden box on which she makes her favorite mayonnaise and tomato sandwiches. She always freely offers to share any food she has with other homeless friends and even those who stop to talk, generously suggesting that, "You can take the first bite. I didn't touch it."

Because of its weight and size, Darian cannot get the cart up over the curb. She keeps it in the street near the cars. This means that as she pushes it slowly up and down the street all day long, she is living almost her entire life directly in traffic. She

A DAY IN THE LIFE OF DARIAN MOORE

stops off along her route to sit or sleep for awhile and to be both stared at as a spectacle and to stare back. Every aspect of her life including sleeping, eating, and going to the bathroom is constantly in public view. With as much modesty as the circumstances allow, she discreetly steps back against a building to change her clothes and finds an empty box to use as a toilet. The busyness of the street provides her with protection, a social life and the perpetual TV-like diversion of watching people pass by. But she has no space to call her own and she never has a moment's privacy. Her privacy, her home, is her cart with all its possessions. In the streets she is vulnerable to attack by thieves who have heard rumors and stories about bag ladies who have thousands of dollars. Periodically they turn over her cart, rifle through her things and rip her clothing off while she is sleeping, to see if she is hiding any money. City children and teenagers either grab things from her cart and go racing away laughing, or throw things at her for entertainment. People passing by in cars shout at her and amuse themselves by trying to lean out of their windows and lift something from her cart.

Middle Eastern men working at a nearby fruit stand often give Darian a piece of watermelon or a peach. One night they walked over to me and asked me why I was with her and why I was taking pictures. They were sympathetic and curious about her. After I explained my project, they proceeded to repeat to me every myth I have ever heard about shopping bag ladies: "That lady don't need nothing. She probably gets a welfare check. If she had a son he would come and get her. No son would leave his mother out like that. If they gave her an apartment she

A DAY IN THE LIFE OF DARIAN MOORE

wouldn't take it, because she's used to being out here. She's really just nuts. She should be locked up. She has a choice and she chooses to stay out on the streets. She's happy there." We talked for a bit about the partial truth of much of what they were saying but I had a hard time explaining the complexity of Darian's existence. She has adapted to living on the street and says herself that she probably could no longer make it on the inside. But just the same, she finds it extremely difficult to live outdoors. Not only is she constantly exposed to the elements but she is also confronted with the condemnation and abuse of many around her. She doesn't like it, but has there ever been any real choice for her?

Darian, like many others, lacks the skill to negotiate the public welfare system. Applying for public assistance is, as one social worker put it, very intensive labor. Women who have been living on the streets for any length of time have often lost all their personal and familial documents such as rent receipts, birth certificates, death certificates, marriage licenses, pay stubs and letters from former employers. Procuring them would require extensive phone calls and research, letter writing, traveling between offices and an ability to comprehend the instructions on forms and applications. Finding one's way through this maze of bureaucratic requirements is taxing even for the young and the stable and healthy. For people in great personal crisis, suffering from physical and emotional infirmities, without friends for support and encouragement, being processed through welfare care can become one task too many to accomplish. Darian has neither the patience nor endurance for rules and

A DAY IN THE LIFE OF DARIAN MOORE

regulations that she perceives as invasive and humiliating. She simply walked out of the welfare office and attempted to fend for herself as best she could on the streets. The outside has now become the known and familiar. For her, it is less dangerous than the SRO's and in a way more private. Perhaps by refusing welfare care and other institutionalized help, she is trying to maintain some level of dignity and control in her life.

Much of what Darian has to say is confusing and incomprehensible. But if one is willing to read between the lines, the insight and clarity she has about her life comes through. —*A.M.R.*

DARIAN MOORE

I wasn't born. I'm heaven sent. I arrived from heaven with my father shot and dead. My mother was dead too. They vaporize when they're dead, so I haven't got a mother or a father forever now. I've had many children, about eighteen children, and I've been married three times with that amnesia. But it's not good to count children. You should only count money. I've been living outside since 1970. Sometimes they shove me off to the Mary House but it's about a billion years passed by.

What is today? Saturday? Oh, Sunday. Well, I missed the whole day. I slept the whole day. I knew I would do that. I went to sleep at three o'clock in the afternoon. I sleep by the bank on Thirteenth Street and Fifth Avenue, but they throw things in the middle of the night. At four o'clock in the morning one of

A DAY IN THE LIFE OF DARIAN MOORE

them got a bunch of envelopes and threw them in my face. They hurt me. I'm not any safer on Sixth Avenue either. They do me in over there too. I try sleeping during the day but I can't stay up at night either.

It's not safe for me to sleep outside at night. Forget it. If they don't kick me, they'll shoot me. I get attacked a lot when I'm sleeping, when they catch me alone. Why do they do it? Well, it started out of jealousy for the simple reason that they don't like a good-looking person.

The kids throw things at me in the doorways. These kids are snotty fucking bastards. Ill mannered. They'll turn around and punch their own mothers and fathers. If they can't have their way they will go out of their way to hurt anybody.

I stay on the streets because I want to, but that's only partly the reason. See, I couldn't trust anybody in an apartment, not after what they've done to me. After that supper party, I gave about forty supper parties, they got a group of machine guns to take me to another country, in another hotel. They raped me there and killed my children. The atheists did it.

When I get up in the morning I like to look at the books I got with me. I read different journals. I have B. Altman's books on linens and silverware. This one is about fashions. House and Gardens. I look at the arrangements of furniture that they make. Of course they'd trip every minute on their heads if they used that kind of arrangement. But you can't tell them anything. I suppose I could write them a letter.

A DAY IN THE LIFE OF DARIAN MOORE

I worked in Macy's during the Christmas rush for five years wrapping packages. I also worked as a waitress for one hour a day on First Avenue for one meal a day. He could only afford to pay me for one hour. Then I worked at Pilgrim State Hospital scrubbing floors, the office floors. But that was before I got shot. After I got shot what could I do with four thousand bullets in my stomach?

I make all my clothes from Simplicity. I didn't learn my sewing. I came with it. I try to sell the things I make and I have them separated from the other things on my push cart. But if they don't buy it they'll steal it. What can you do?

Home relief don't give me a check. They don't want to know nothing. Like I wrote for it but they didn't give it to me. They gave it to the woman I had the child with and then they terminated it. I made four applications and he told me like this, "Go up to the fifth floor. You have to fill out another application." When I heard that I walked out because there are people who go in the same day and get the check the same day. Every check comes out of that floor but he was trying to give me some story. They like to make a fool out of you, so I walked out.

This is how they fixed me. If I get a flat then they'll send me a check. Now where am I going to get a flat? They gave me a room in a hotel once but they took the two checks that I gave them. Then they threw me out the second day because Betty's brother was in there. I made sure they mailed the checks back to welfare but when you move they terminate the checks. You have to have a

A DAY IN THE LIFE OF DARIAN MOORE

steady place because they know it screws people up in the hotel one way or another. They just don't trust me in a hotel.

You see, because I'm in and out all the time I don't know when to change my clothes. I wash my hair by putting lotion on it and getting a towel or a piece of blanket. Then I wipe it until the grease comes off. I put alcohol on it, that gets the cream out right away. Once every six months I get two cups of hot water from the restaurant and douse it with that. Washes it right off and I don't use no soap on it.

The doctors and physicians know how to cut and control the brain because brains is power. But I keep fighting them. They're pulling the veins in my heart. They're pulling the heart strings but I'm a doctor too. I have this medicine to stop the pain. I just put it on the skin and it helps. It's Anacin, Bayer Aspirin, and Tylenol all stomped on and mixed together in cold cream and two different kinds of lotion.

When I get the pain, that's okay because I get a dollar and I get dimes and keep calling. I keep calling randomly. I dial the numbers, any numbers and talk to who I get. It doesn't matter. It's better to call that way, to dial out into the universe and see what you get. That way you know you get what you should.

Where do I go in the winter when it gets cold outside? I stand outside like everybody else.

HOUSING DIRECTORY

The following list is by no means complete. Some residences did not want to be listed because they are already overcrowded. Others asked that their addresses be eliminated because they house battered women. Many of these places listed do not provide shelter, but do offer free food, clothing or counseling. Some charge a fee. Others have special requirements for acceptance including participation in religious services, alcoholism treatment programs and therapy programs, or are for battered women only. It is always best to call first whenever possible. If a center is full or does not provide shelter they can often suggest other places to try.

DECATUR, ALABAMA

CRISIS CALL CENTER
Mental Health Center
Highway 31 South at Flint
(P.O. Box 637)
205-355-8000

MONTGOMERY, ALABAMA

FAITH RESCUE MISSION
108 Camden Street
205-262-6024
Two nights if the person
  has a social security card

SALVATION ARMY
900 Bell Street
205-265-0281
One night every 30 days

PHOENIX, ARIZONA

ALCOHOL TURNING POINT HOME
  FOR WOMEN
3702 North 13th Avenue
602-274-0730
AA and NA
Homey atmosphere for adult females
Must be sober for 24 hours

COMMUNITY INFORMATION
  AND REFERRAL SERVICES
(24-hour telephone service)
602-263-8856

RAINBOW RETREAT
43-32 N. 12th Street
602-263-1113
Specializing in alcoholism,
  children and crisis

SALVATION ARMY
801 West Jefferson
602-256-5959
Free food and shelter

ST. VINCENT DEPAUL
119 South 9th Avenue
602-243-4121
Hot meal served at noon

SOJOURNER CENTER
357 North 4th Avenue
602-258-5344
Crisis counseling
  for female ex-offenders

TOBY HOUSE
303 West Willeta Street
602-257-1271
Rehabilitation for former
  mental patients

TUMBLEWEED HOUSE
309 West Portland
602-271-9849
For teenagers only

LITTLE ROCK, ARKANSAS

SALVATION ARMY WELFARE
  AND TRANSIENT LODGE
1111 W. Markham
501-374-9296

UNION MISSION
Cantrell Road
501-375-4459

EL CAJON, CALIFORNIA

EAST COUNTY SHELTER
165 Rea Avenue
714-447-2428

SAN DIEGO, CALIFORNIA

BIG SISTER'S LEAGUE
714-297-1172
Fee charged

CASA DE PAS
714-234-3164
For battered women only

SALVATION ARMY EMERGENCY LODGE
825 7th Avenue Main
714-239-6221

SO. EAST EMERGENCY LODGE
4996 Holly Street
714-263-9286
Temporary shelter for
  women and families

SAN FRANCISCO, CALIFORNIA

HAIGHT-ASHBURY SWITCHBOARD
1539 Haight near Ashbury
415-387-7000
People's information
  and referral center
Crash pad

NATIONAL COUNCIL ON
  ALCOHOLISM
2131 Union Street
415-563-5400
24 hour information
  and referrals to alcoholism
  services; some counseling

RAPHAEL HOUSE
1065 Sutter near Larkin
415-474-4621
Shelter, meals and supportive
  atmosphere for women and families
  Call first

S. F. NIGHT MINISTRY
(Telephone service only)
415-986-1464
10 pm-4 am
Limited emergency housing
  for women and families

S. F. WOMEN'S SWITCHBOARD
3543 18th Street
415-431-1414
Mon.-Sat. Noon to 8 pm
Women's information referrals

FREE FOOD ONLY, SAN FRANCISCO

FAMILY SERVICES
101 Valencia Street
415-861-0755
8:30 am-4 pm Mon-Fri. Closed 12-1
Referrals

GLIDE CHURCH
330 Ellis Street near Taylor
415-771-6300
Free meals 6 pm Mondays only

HOSPITALITY HOUSE
146 Leavenworth Street near Turk
415-776-2103
10 am-6 pm, Mon thru Fri.
Various aids and referrals and counseling

LIFELINE MISSION
917 Folsom near 5th Street
415-392-2220
M, T, Th, F, Sat 8:30-9:30 am;
  6:30 pm
Religious service

MISSION ALCOHOLIC CENTER
1175 Howard Street near 8th Street
415-621-6471
7 am-11 pm
Alcoholism information and help

ONE MIND TEMPLE
351 Divisadero near Oak
415-621-4054
Wed. 11-12:30 pm, Sun. 11-2:00 pm
Vegetarian meal

OZANAM CENTER
(St. Vincent de Paul)
1175 Howard Street near 8th Street
415-864-3057
Drop-in counseling, coffee, clothing

ST. ANTHONY'S DINING ROOM
(AND CLINIC)
45 Jones near Market
415-864-0241
Mon-Sat 11 am-12:30 pm

SALVATION ARMY HARBOR LIGHT
1275 Harrison Street
415-864-7000
24 hrs. 7 days
Alcoholism information and help

S. F. GOSPEL MISSION
221 6th Street near Howard
415-495-7366
Mon-Sat 7:30 pm
Religious service

LONG BEACH, CALIFORNIA

WOMEN'S SHELTER
714-437-4663

SANTA MONICA, CALIFORNIA

SALVATION ARMY
Adult Rehab. Center
213-450-7235

SANTA MONICA DEPARTMENT
OF SOCIAL SERVICES
213-974-1234
After 5 pm

SUN LIGHT MISSION
1754 14th Street
213-450-8802
For families with children

SAN PEDRO, CALIFORNIA

Y.W.C.A.
714-547-9343
For battered women

DENVER, COLORADO

BRANDON HOUSE
Volunteers of America
1260 Pennsylvania Avenue
303-832-7826

CATHOLIC WORKER
2420 Welton Street
303-573-8830

SACRED HEART HOUSE
2844 Lawrence
303-534-4268

SALVATION ARMY
2145 Larimer
303-573-1606

HARTFORD, CONNECTICUT

THE BRIDGE
West Hartford, Connecticut
203-521-6890
For teenagers only

CENTER CITY CHURCHES
170 Main Street
203-728-3201
Free food (various locations)

COMMUNITY RENEWAL TEAM
203-278-9950
Free food

FRIENDSHIP CENTER
Run by Center City Churches, Inc.
203-249-8443
Free food

INTERVAL HOUSE, INC.
203-246-9149
For battered women
and their children.
Emergency service
hot line: 203-527-0550
Battered women emergency
support service: 203-249-0501

SALVATION ARMY EMERGENCY SHELTER
855 Asylum Avenue
203-525-1898

ST. ELIZABETH HOUSE
118 Main Street
203-246-5643
Boarding home and rooming house
No children
Fee charged

PUTNAM HOT LINE AND SHELTER
203-774-2020
24-hour crisis intervention services
For battered women only.

Y.W.C.A.
135 Broad Street
203-525-1163
One or two rooms for emergencies only

YOUTH SERVICES
203-646-6500
For teenagers only

MERIDEN/WALLINGFORD, CONNECTICUT

HOT LINE AND SHELTER
203-238-1501
For battered women only

NEW BRITAIN, CONNECTICUT

PRUDENCE CRANDALL
HOT LINE AND SHELTER
203-225-6357
For battered women only

NEW LONDON, CONNECTICUT

HOT LINE AND SHELTER
203-447-0366
For battered women only

MIAMI, FLORIDA

MIAMI SWITCHBOARD
305-358-4357

NEW OPPORTUNITY HOUSE
777 N.W. 30th Street
305-638-6620
Fee charged for shared room
and two meals

OPEN HOUSE FOUNDATION
1566 S.W. First Street
305-621-1697
Fee charged for room
and board

SALVATION ARMY WOMAN'S LODGE
1398 S.W. First Street
305-643-4902

WOMEN IN DISTRESS
Salvation Army
122 N.E. 24th Street
302-643-4900
Maximum two week stay
Meals and room

WOMEN'S FELLOWSHIP
ASSOCIATION RESCUE HOME
1290 N.W. 36th Street
305-634-1164
Fee charged

WOODS HALFWAY HOUSE
189 N.E. 26th Street
305-573-7109
Fee charged

CHICAGO, ILLINOIS

BRAXTON HOUSE
100834 S. Perry
312-264-1183
Geriatric and mental
health referrals

CHICAGO ABUSED WOMEN
COALITION
312-786-9013
For battered women

CHRIST HOUSE
6140 N. Winthrop
312-262-2781

CHRIST TEMPLE
9248 S. Cottage Grove
312-874-3038
Fee charged

DEPARTMENT OF HUMAN SERVICES
312-744-5829

HOUSING DIRECTORY

FAIRFAX HOUSE
135 S. Central Park
312-533-3656
Fee charged

GOSPEL LEAGUE HOME
955 W. Grand Avenue
312-943-2480
For women and children only

HOUSE OF GOOD SHEPHERD
312-935-3434
For battered women

JACKSON VIEW HOTEL
3501 W. Jackson Street
312-638-1644
Fee charged

PACIFIC GARDEN MISSION
646 S. State Street
312-922-1463
For families

POVERBLO HOUSE
1338 N. Ashland
312-252-5160

SAHARA HOUSE
312-539-7795
For battered women

ST. ELIZABETH'S
7635 N. Bosworth
312-465-3250

SALVATION ARMY EMERGENCY LODGE
800 West Lawrence Street
312-275-9383

URBAN PROGRESS CENTERS
  AND MOBILE UNITS
312-744-8004
Community services

DES MOINES, IOWA

BETHEL MISSION
954 6th Street
515-244-5445
Free food for women

CATHOLIC WORKER HOUSE
713 Indiana
515-243-0763

DOOR OF FAITH MISSION
1006 Grand
515-282-0208

FIRST CALL FOR HELP
United Way Agency
700 6th Avenue
515-244-8646
Not a shelter
Advice and counseling

HAWTHORNE HILL
921 Pleasant
515-283-1911

SALVATION ARMY
City Headquarters
515-288-8554

SALVATION ARMY SOCIAL SERVICES
1326 6th Avenue
515-283-0131
Not a shelter Welfare-type services

Y.W.C.A.
717 Grand Avenue
515-244-8961

FORT DODGE, IOWA

POLICE STATION
Central Avenue
515-576-1168
Will house people for one night

SALVATION ARMY
501 Central Avenue
515-576-1281

TOPEKA, KANSAS

RESCUE MISSION
605 North Kansas Avenue
913-354-1744
For women and families

SALVATION ARMY
913-233-9648

LEXINGTON, KENTUCKY

BATTERED WOMEN'S ABUSE SHELTER
606-255-9808
For battered women only

SALVATION ARMY
736 West Main Street
606-252-7706

BATON ROUGE, LOUISIANA

VOLUNTEERS OF AMERICA
827 America
504-387-2267
Temporary shelter
Usually overnight

NEW ORLEANS, LOUISIANA

WOMEN'S LODGE
112 6th Street
504-895-6611

PORTLAND, MAINE

SALVATION ARMY
207-774-6304

WELFARE DEPARTMENT
207-774-6304

Y.W.C.A.
Spring Street
Fee charged

BALTIMORE, MARYLAND

BALTIMORE RESCUE MISSION
4 North Central Avenue
301-342-2533

EMERGENCY SERVICES CENTER
1510 Gilford Avenue
1114 North Calvert Street
301-685-8878
Small fee charged

HOUSE OF RUTH
301-889-7884
For battered women only

BOSTON, MASSACHUSETTS

CASA MYRNA DASQUEZ
P.O. Box 18014
For battered women only

CHARDON ST. HOME
41 New Chardon Street
A few beds for single women

ELIZABETH STONE HALL
108 Brookside Avenue
For battered women
Fee charged

HARBORLIGHTS
407 Shawmut Avenue
617-536-7469

PINE STREET
60 Briston Street
617-482-4944
50 beds

ROSIE'S PLACE
1662 Washington Street
617-536-5351
Free meals at 5 pm
Beds

SANTA MARIA HOUSE
11 Waltham Street
617-423-4366

CAMBRIDGE, MASSACHUSETTS

THE SHELTER
P.O. Box 516
617-547-1885

TRANSITION HOUSE
617-661-7203
For battered women
Small fee

SOMMERVILLE, MASSACHUSETTS

RESPOND
617-623-5900
For battered women only

DORCHESTER, MASSACHUSETTS

WOMEN'S INC.
570 Warren Street
617-442-6166
Battered women,
    drug/alcohol counseling

SPRINGFIELD, MASSACHUSETTS

HAMPDEN COUNTY WOMEN'S CENTER
764 Alden Street
413-783-4004
24-hour hot line

INFORMATION REFERRAL SERVICE
United Way
413-737-2691

SALVATION ARMY
413-785-1921

Y.W.C.A.
135 State Street
413-732-3121

WESTFIELD, MASSACHUSETTS

HEGIRA
Association for the support
    of human services
42 Arnold Street
413-568-0966
Emergency shelter

WILBRAHAM, MASSACHUSETTS

HEART HOUSE
P.O. Box 764
413-737-5697
By referral only
    for battered women

DETROIT, MICHIGAN

CAPUCHIAN
313-579-1330
Free food and clothing

HEARTLINE
8201 Sylvester Street
313-923-4200
Must be working or in school
Single women only
Permanent residence for up to one year

MANNA COMMUNITY MEALS
St. Peter's Episcopal Church
Corner of Trumbull
    and Michigan Avenue
Free food

RAINBOW SHELTER
138 Pingel Street
313-872-9550
Take people on S.S.I.
    or welfare

DAY HOUSE
2640 Trumbull
313-963-4539
For women and families

DAY HOUSE
Central Emergency Shelter
313-256-1695
Must fit emergency need
    requirements

EMERGENCY SHELTER
Salvation Army
1331 Trumbull
313-962-2100

EVANGELINE CENTER
1331 Trumbal
313-961-2292
Women and their families

COMMUNITY INFORMATION SERVICES
United Community Services
51 W. Warren
313-833-3430

CROSS ROADS
4800 Woodward
313-831-2000
Social service agency

LA BELLE
La Belle Street
313-867-1525

ST. VINCENT DE PAUL
313-273-2200

FERNDALE, MICHIGAN

HOSPITALITY HOUSE
814 W. 9-Mile Road
313-398-6955
Temporary shelter
    for Oakland County only
For women and their families

DULUTH, MINNESOTA

BATTERED WOMEN'S COALITION
    (OR RELIGIOUS WOMEN'S COALITION)
P.O. Box 3205
218-728-3679

HILLCREST HOUSE
1230 E. 9th
218-728-4291

SALVATION ARMY
Family Services
118 N. 3rd Avenue, West
218-722-7367

ST. PAUL, MINNESOTA

BOOTH HOUSE
Run by the Salvation Army
1471 Como Avenue West
612-646-2601

KANSAS CITY, MISSOURI

JEFFERSON HOME
308 Garfield
816-471-0149
For women and children
Must be referred
    by another agency

PILGRIM HOUSE
551 Forest Street
816-474-9380

SALVATION ARMY
Emergency Lodge
101 West Lindwood
816-756-1455
For women
    and their families

BUTTE, MONTANA

DOYLE'S MISSION
1204 E. 2nd Street
406-792-5394

LINCOLN, NEBRASKA

PEOPLE'S CITY MISSION
124 South 9th Street
402-475-1303
Family shelter connected
    with the Salvation Army

ALBUQUERQUE, NEW MEXICO

BROTHERS OF GOOD SHEPHERD
505-243-2527

HAVEN OF LOVE
425 Isleta S.W.
Fee charged

SALVATION ARMY
400 John Street S.E.
Eight beds

SANTA FE, NEW MEXICO

SALVATION ARMY
525 W. Alemeda
505-988-8054
Food in special cases
No shelter

NEW YORK CITY, NEW YORK

BOWERY MISSION
227 Bowery
212-674-3456
Meals at 12 and 7:30 pm

HOUSING DIRECTORY

CONTACT
316 East 10th Street
212-533-3570
Medical and legal aid,
   employment information
   and housing program
Especially for runaways
   aged 12-17

COVENANT HOUSE
260 West 44th Street
212-354-4323
Live-in for runaways
   and kids passing through
   the city. First
   come, first serve
For girls 14-17

DWELLING PLACE
409 West 40th Street
212-564-7887
Shelter and food

EMERGENCY ASSISTANCE UNIT
241 Church Street
212-344-5241
Temporary assistance

EVERYTHING FOR EVERYBODY
131 Avenue B
212-477-4500
Free meals 10 am-4 pm,
   7 days a week
Free clothing 8 am-8 pm,
   low cost housing
Members and non-members

GRACE AND HOPE MISSION
114-116 Third Avenue
212-982-1230
Religious service
   followed by a lunch
   8 pm-9 pm (Closed Mon.)

MARY HOUSE
(Catholic Worker)
55 East 3rd Street
212-777-9617
Meals daily at 11:30 am-5:30 pm
Must call first
Permanent residence

MORAVIAN CHURCH
154 Lexington Avenue
212-683-4219
Coffee pot drop-in center

NEW YORK CITY DEPARTMENT
OF SOCIAL SERVICES
Yorkville Special Services
225 East 34th Street
212-725-4086
Assistance with transportation
   home to anyone stranded in N.Y.C.
   who has a permanent residence
   elsewhere
Temporary maintenance also

NEW YORK DEPARTMENT
OF SOCIAL SERVICES
Maternity Shelter Care
80 Lafayette Street
212-433-3573
Pre-natal residential care for
   pregnant unmarried women and
   counseling for single parents

PUBLIC BATHS
133 Allen Street
212-473-9728
Free showers Tues.-Sat. 9:30 am-4:30 pm
Bring your own soap and towel

SHELTER CARE CENTER FOR WOMEN
350 Lafayette Street
212-460-1176
Temporary home for women
Must be a resident
   to receive food, showers,
   counseling and medical care

ST. FRANCIS BREAD LINE
136 West 31st Street
212-736-8500
Sandwiches and coffee
   given out at 6:45 am

STAR OF THE SEA
145-53 South Road
Jamaica, Queens
212-523-1088

THE DOOR
618 Avenue of the Americas
212-691-6161
Mon.-Thurs. 6-10 pm
Legal, medical and housing
   information for youths
   up to 21 years

WEST SIDE CLUSTER
Tony Olivieri Center
257 West 30th Street
212-947-3211
Free food for women

WESTSIDE CRISIS UNIT
216 West 102 Street
212-222-1171
Short-term therapy
   on a sliding scale
Serving people from 94th to 110th Street

WOMEN'S SURVIVAL SPACE
Bay Ridge, Brooklyn
212-439-7281
For battered women

FARGO, NORTH DAKOTA

SALVATION ARMY
Community Center
304 Roberts Avenue
701-232-5565

Y.W.C.A.
411 Broadway
701-232-2547
Emergency housing for women

MINOT, NORTH DAKOTA

AREA SOCIAL SERVICE CENTER
400 22nd N.W.
701-852-1251

CONCERNED LOW INCOME PEOPLE
   (C.L.I.P.)
2001 Valker Road
701-839-7221

COPPEN HOME
Family Guidance Institute
400 22nd Avenue N.W.
701-839-7221
Battered women, unwed mothers

Y.W.C.A.
205 3rd Avenue S.E.
701-838-1726

CINCINNATI, OHIO

EMERGENCY HOME CLIENT
513-762-9215
Part of the Salvation Army

SALVATION ARMY
3595 Washington Avenue
513-751-6900

WOMEN HELPING WOMEN
9th Street & Walnut Street
513-381-5610
Counseling and referral
   services only

Y.W.C.A.
Butler County Agency
513-863-7099
Crisis shelter for battered women

HAMILTON, OHIO

SALVATION ARMY
235 Ludlow Street
513-863-1445

Y.W.C.A.
244 Dayton Street
Fee charged

OXFORD, OHIO

TOGETHER, INC.
14 So. Campus Street
513-523-4146
24-hour hot line

HARRISBURG, PENNSYLVANIA

SALVATION ARMY
1122 Reen Street
717-233-6755
Not a shelter

Y.W.C.A.
717-234-6221
Fee charged

PHILADELPHIA, PENNSYLVANIA

MERCY HOSPICE
334 S. 13th Street
215-545-5153
For families and children

PEOPLE'S EMERGENCY
3311 Chestnut Street
215-382-7522
Open only on weekends

SAINT RITA'S
1231 Broad Street
215-468-8700

SALVATION ARMY
715 North Broad
215-787-2876

MEMPHIS, TENNESSEE

SALVATION ARMY
200 Munroe
901-526-1066
Women, children and families

TRAVELER'S AIDE
46 N. 3rd Street
901-525-5466

NASHVILLE, TENNESSEE

NASHVILLE UNION RESCUE MISSION
7th and Demounbreum Street
615-256-7215

SALVATION ARMY
600 Demounbreum Street
615-242-0412
Food and shelter

DALLAS, TEXAS

FIRST PRESBYTERIAN CHURCH
Corner of Harwood and Wood
214-748-8051

SALVATION ARMY
2203 N. Akard
214-742-9131
Temporary shelter

HOUSTON, TEXAS

HOUSTON CHRISTIAN MISSION
5069 Calhoun Street
713-741-1174

SALVATION ARMY
713-222-8248
Welfare services

SALVATION ARMY TEMPORARY
   RESIDENCE FOR WOMEN
   AND CHILDREN
416 McGowan
713-228-1505

SANTA MARIA HOTEL
1217 Paschal Street
713-223-3806

STEPPING STONES
1902 West Lamar
713-528-8426
For alcoholic women

TRAVELER'S AIDE
Alston Street
713-522-3846

WOMEN'S CHRISTIAN HOME
310 Pacific Street
713-523-7809
Food, lodging
   and medical attention

SAN ANTONIO, TEXAS

SALVATION ARMY
226 Nolan Street
512-226-2291

TRAVELER'S AIDE
512-226-7181

UNITED WAY INFORMATION
   AND REFERRAL SERVICE
512-227-H.E.L.P.
Hot line

WASHINGTON, D.C.

CENTRAL UNION MISSION
613 C Street N.W.
202-628-4349
No children

DEBORAH'S PLACE
1327 M Street N.W.
Women over 18, no children

EMERGENCY FAMILY SHELTER
1531 P Street N.W.
202-673-7694
No single adults with children

EMERGENCY HOUSE OF RUTH
651 10th Street N.E.
202-547-2600

FLORENCE CRITTENDOM HOME
1459 Reservoir Road N.W.
202-333-3600
For pregnant and homeless women

HOUSE OF IMOGEN
214 P Street N.W.
202-797-7460
Battered women
Children occasionally

MY SISTER'S PLACE
202-529-5991
For battered women only

PARKSIDE
1336 I Street N.W.
202-727-0845

PARKSIDE HOTEL
122 C Street N.W.
202-727-9672

SARAH'S HOUSE
1335 N Street N.W.
202-232-6167

WOMEN'S AND CHILDREN'S
   EMERGENCY SHELTER
504 15th N.W.
202-783-4058

ZAZZHAUS HOUSE
1320 Street N.W.
202-232-9533

MADISON, WISCONSIN

COMMUNITY INFORMATION
   AND REFERRAL
(Information)
210 Monona Avenue
608-266-6366

SALVATION ARMY
608-256-2321
Vouchers to the Y.W.C.A.

UPPER ROOM
114 W. Mifflin
608-255-4894

CHEYENNE, WYOMING

SALVATION ARMY
307-634-7890
Will put up people
   for one night in a motel

HOUSING DIRECTORY